The Complete Book of

TAPESTRY WEAVING

The Complete Book of

TAPESTRY WEAVING

ALEC PEARSON

St. Martin's Press, New York

For Brigitte

The front jacket illustration is of 'Variations on a tarn',
by Alec Pearson, 180cm × 150cm (6ft × 5ft)

The back jacket illustration is of 'Roads into a village',
165cm × 120cm (5ft × 4ft)

THE COMPLETE BOOK OF TAPESTRY WEAVING. Copyright © 1984
by Alec Pearson. All rights reserved. Printed in the United
States of America. No part of this book may be used or
reproduced in any manner whatsoever without written
permission except in the case of brief quotations embodied
in critical articles or reviews. For information, address
St. Martin's Press, 175 Fifth Avenue, New York, N.Y. 10010.

Library of Congress Cataloging in Publication Data

Pearson, Alec.
 The complete book of tapestry weaving

 1. Tapestry. 2. Hand weaving. I. Title.
TT849. P43 1984   746.3   83–21189
ISBN 0–312–15633–2

First published in Great Britain in 1984 by Batsford Books.
First U.S. Edition
10 9 8 7 6 5 4 3 2 1

Printed in United Kingdom

CONTENTS

ACKNOWLEDGEMENTS

Black and white photographs

Photographers: Foto Lore Bermbach, Düsseldorf, figures 10, 22, 33–52, 67, 69, 74–79, 82, 83, 89, 93–114, 132, 134–138; Kate Grillet, Cambridge, figures 74, 80; James Austin, Cambridge, figures 70, 139, 140, 141; Owners of tapestries reproduced in black and white: Abbot Hall Art Gallery, Kendal, figure 82; The Chairman, Courtaulds Limited, London, figure 83; All Saints Chapel, Middlesex Polytechnic, figure 112; IBM United Kingdom Limited, figure 131; Guildhall School of Music and Drama, Barbican, London, figure 132; Equitable Life Assurance Society, London, figure 133. Figures 100, 101, 102, 109 are privately owned in the UK; figure 103 is privately owned in the U.S.A.; figure 104 is privately owned in Germany.

Colour photographs

Photographers: James Austin, Cambridge, the front and back jacket colour photographs, 'Variations on a tarn' and 'Roads into a village'; Courtaulds Ltd, 'Landscape by a lake'.

Owners of tapestries reproduced in colour: The Chairman, Courtaulds Ltd, London, 'Landscape by a lake'; private owners in the U.K., 'Village in hills', 'Lake, hills and sea' and 'Towards the sea'; Queen Mary's School, Lytham, Lancs., 'Sand, hills and sea'; private owner in Switzerland, 'Scottish landscape'.

All line illustrations and paintings are by the author.

Note on tapestry dimensions
Throughout the book height is always given before width.

INTRODUCTION

We do not know exactly how tapestry weaving arose in the West, and whether or not there was a clear connection with Coptic weaving. We do know that early sources, during the Gothic period, for designs for tapestry weavers to work from, were miniature paintings, found in mediaeval manuscripts. There are records of both high and low warp looms in use in France in the twelfth and thirteenth centuries, and of payments to painters for designs or cartoons to be used by the weavers. Gothic tapestries are impressive and important. They were simply conceived, even through they include a great amount of detail in trees, flowers, animals and in the garments of the cleanly delineated and well placed figures.

Only fifteen to twenty colours were available originally. The weft was limited to wool, until gold, silver and silk came into use. The warp was spaced from four to eleven ends per centimetre. Limited means often help an artist to concentrate on a balance of form, tone and colour. (In tapestry weaving, too wide a choice can lead to an over-emphasis on brilliant effects and clever techniques. Around the middle of the nineteenth century the Gobelin weavers had over fourteen thousand tones available and were, unfortunately, able to direct their efforts towards close imitation of paintings, rather than to the production of tapestries which grew from the stimulus of painters.)

During the pre-Renaissance period weavers were attached to centres, or moved about in groups. They were allowed much more freedom of interpretation than was permitted later, particularly in the way they used the available colours. We can only speculate that, because all the visual arts were on an equal footing, there was an easy relationship between painter and weaver, neither feeling subservient to the other. The cartoons were often sketches on cloth, lightly coloured, handed on, used freely, the weaver respecting the painter's understanding of composition, and his ability as a draughtsman and colourist, but also valuing his own imaginative skills as a weaver; the painter acknowledging the weaver's right to use his design, and not merely to copy it.

With the coming of the Renaissance this changed. We can trace the deterioration of the position of the weaver from freedom, to supervised interpretation, to strict and highly skilled imitation, during the classical period. The Italian Renaissance established the fine artists above other visual artists, in a position of superiority. The decline began to set in for the tapestry weaver, as an artist-craftsman, when Pope Leo X ordered tapestries from Brussels to be made from cartoons by Raphael, illustrating The Acts of the Apostles. The aim was to imitate closely the painted cartoons.

My particular purpose here is not to examine individual tapestries, nor to study the various centres, but to note the changing relationship between tapestry weaver and painter. As finer and more closely spaced warps and finer yarns for wefts were used, the deterioration in what we should call creative tapestry, from the weaver's point of view, continued until the 1930s. Even as late as 1933, tapestries which were close copies of paintings by famous modern painters of the time, were the norm. This industry is still active, of course, but the point to keep in mind is that in the 1930s there was little else going on. Apart, that is, from the experiments of Jean Lurçat, the French artist, who had been working since 1916 on cross stitch experiments and who, in 1939, initiated co-operation with the weavers of Aubusson, together with a few other artists. They began to work in close touch with the weavers, restricting the number of colours and simplifying the designs, so that the weavers could execute the work at the speed of the weavers of the eleventh and twelfth centuries, when about two square metres per month was possible. In 1945 Lurçat and others founded an Association of Tapestry Cartoon-Painters. Four basic rules were agreed about modern tapestry:

1 It should be woven in its own right and not be merely a copy of a picture.

2 It should suit the room or building for which it is intended.

3 Any cartoon, or preliminary drawing, should be the same size as the tapestry.

4 It should be of relatively coarse weave, which means not more than 12 ends per inch.

Since then many artists have worked for tapestry workshops and a growing number have, in their own studios, become both painter and weaver.

The Book of Tapestry by Pierre Verlet, Michel Florisoone, Adolf Hoffmeister and Francois Tabard, and *Tapestry, Mirror of History* by F. P. Thomson, give interesting information about historical and modern tapestry and the making of tapestries. Both are well illustrated.

Contemporary tapestry designers and weavers are working in several areas, and not always in exclusive groupings. The activities often overlap, but it is necessary to make some distinctions, in order to understand some of the attitudes which are prevalent today. In the first group are weavers of flat tapestries, who think like painters. Then, but not in any order of priority or superiority, are weavers who think three-dimensionally, like sculptors. And there are weavers of flat tapestries, who think like weavers, and have usually studied weaving as a main subject. Fibre artists think two- and three-dimensionally, in terms of threads, fibres, techniques, ideas which can not be tied to either painting or sculpture. People in this group are not always weavers in the strict sense of the word, but may use adhesives, may sew, or embroider, in a wide range of materials. There are environmental weavers, who think like interior architects. And there are some who might be called performance weavers, who create public events which involve textiles.

The history of art is sometimes presented as a ladder, with certain selected individuals and groups of artists gathered on each conveniently dated rung. But it has also been described as a wheel, or a number of wheels, on which artists are working along different spokes. Although the ladder version is favoured among those writers on art, artists and arts administrators, who are assembled on the rung dated 1980s, the wheel is a more accurate description of what is actually happening among artists all over the world. This is true of weaving, and of textiles in general. A great deal of varied work is being done, contemporary and authentic, because it springs from individuals, and motivates individuals, who are alive and active today.

This book explores some aspects of one spoke of the wheel, in which tapestry weaving is closely related to drawing and painting, and where the methods and ideas explained are those used in my own studio. The illustrations are, for the most part, landscapes involving hills and lakes, which are what I find most important in my own life and work. The techniques, materials and terminology are not always orthodox. For example, most tapestry weavers recommend corded cotton for the warp, especially for beginners. As I have always used linen, and have not found it to be disadvantageous for students, cotton is only mentioned in passing. Terminology is not over-emphasised, but it is recognised that there is an argument in favour of standard terms at all times. As these are not necessarily used in the text, the glossary makes specific reference to them. There are occasional notes and references, in the text and in the book list, to techniques and ideas outside the main thesis of this book, which have been included to guide those who would like to use a finer warp than the one I normally use.

Ideally, Chapters 1 and 2 should be used side by side. Drawing and tapestry weaving are concurrent activities, and if you are hesitant about drawing, as many weavers are, the sooner you become engaged in the excitement of making your own drawings the better. Too great an involvement in weaving techniques, for their own sake, will subdue the vigour of the ideas which come from your drawings. The aim in presenting this book of tapestry weaving is not to cover everything, but to make a well-balanced start, in which the tapestry weaver is also the artist and, as a result therefore, the innovator rather than the imitator.

1 A TECHNIQUE FOR WOVEN TAPESTRY

Basic equipment and materials

The loom, warp and weft
a frame or loom, minimum size 50 cm × 60 cm
 (1 ft 8 in × 2 ft)
two cops 10/6 linen rug warp
2/5s rug yarn in white, light grey, medium grey,
 dark grey, and natural black
tape measure (metal expanding type preferred,
 but dressmakers' tape measure is adequate)
large black felt pen or marker
large plastic set square 45°
scissors or shears
wooden strips, as long as the width of the
 loom × 25 mm × 5 mm (× 1 in × $\frac{1}{4}$ in)
cardboard strips 4 cm (1$\frac{1}{2}$ in) wide
cartridge paper, pencil, masking tape, when full-
 size cartoon of tapestry is required

Dyeing
hot and cold water supply
gas or electric heating supply
stainless steel bucket or bowl
hot water chemical dyes (Dylon) in a small range
 of colours
salt
string

Finishing and hanging (included here, but dealt
with in Chapter 3)
furnishing webbing 5 cm (2 in) wide
Velcro 2 cm or 5 cm ($\frac{3}{4}$ in or 2 in) wide

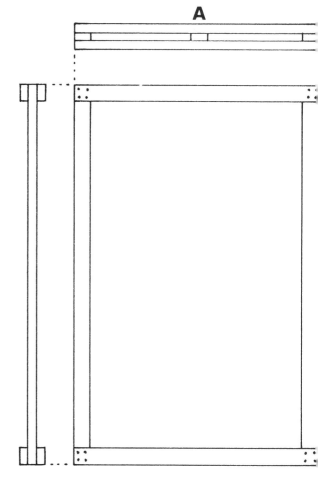

1 Simple tapestry frame

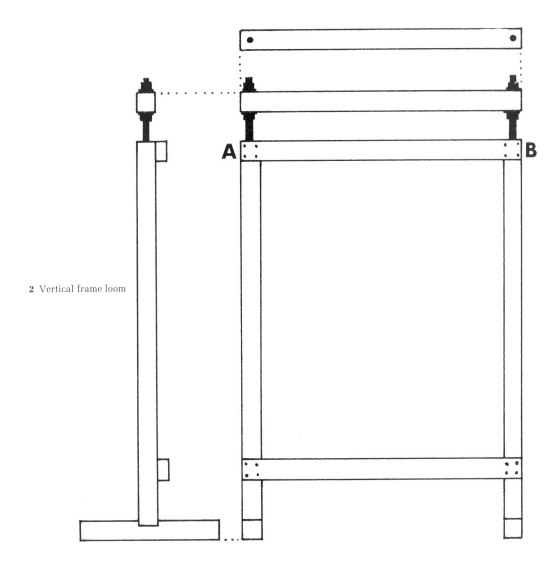

2 Vertical frame loom

A

B

linen or cotton thread
various needles
wooden dowel, or stainless steel rods, or
   aluminium strip 5 cm (2 in) wide
impact adhesive
fishing line (about 11 kg, 23 lb breaking strain)
screwdriver
wall nails or screws
tenon saw
hack saw
hand or electric drill and drills, including
   masonry drill
scissors

The loom

Any horizontal or vertical loom can be used for tapestry weaving. Any frame, including a strong picture frame, is a suitable support for a warp. The basic equipment can, therefore, be expensive or very cheap. Two easily constructed, vertical frame looms, are described in this section, one with a fixed warp where the possibility of varying the tension is limited, and the other with a system for raising or lowering the top cross piece, in order to vary the warp tension.

The first (figure 1), a simple frame, on which a

tapestry 45 cm (1 ft 6 in) wide and up to 100 cm (3 ft 3 in) in length can be made, requires two pieces of wood 90 cm × 5 cm × 2.5 cm (3 ft × 2 in × 1 in) for uprights, and four pieces 60 cm × 5 cm × 2.5 cm (2 ft × 2 in × 1 in) for cross pieces.

Assemble these as illustrated, using two screws and glue for each corner. Glue, additionally, two strengthening blocks of wood, each 10 cm × 5 cm × 2.5 cm (4 in × 2 in × 1 in) at the top and bottom in position A. Good quality, knot-free, pine, is adequate.

This frame can be propped against a wall, held on the lap, and angled against a table, or given feet made from two pieces of wood, each 45 cm × 5 cm × 5 cm (1 ft 6 in × 2 in × 2 in), screwed under the frame at right angles to the cross pieces.

This type of frame can, of course, be wider and longer. For a 180 cm × 240 cm (6 ft × 8 ft) frame, wood about 8 cm × 4 cm or even 5 cm (3 in × 1$\frac{1}{2}$ in or even 2 in) should be used.

The second frame, which is a vertical loom (figure 2), has a cross piece at the top, which can be raised or lowered by means of nuts on the metal studding at each side (figure 3). (Studding is also referred to in ironmongers as 'threaded rod' or 'all-thread' and can be in steel or brass.) The proportions can be varied, according to the size of tapestry required, but a minimum width of 90 cm (3 ft) is recommended, so that a tapestry 75 cm (2 ft 6 in) wide can be woven. This allows for the width of the uprights and a margin of 2.5 cm (1 in) on each side of the tapestry. Fix two uprights 120 cm × 5 cm × 5 cm (4 ft × 2 in × 2 in), as illustrated in figure 2, to two cross pieces, each 90 cm × 5 cm × 2.5 cm (3 ft × 2 in × 1 in), one at the top front, the other at the front, 15 cm (6 in) from the bottom. Be particularly careful with corners A and B. Glue firmly and avoid placing screws which would impede the fixing of the metal studding. The metal studding, 1.5 cm diameter, is 25 cm (10 in) in length, and should have two nuts and two washers. It may be necessary to buy one piece 50 cm in length, which can be cut with a hacksaw. Drill the holes for the studding carefully so that the cross piece, which slides over the

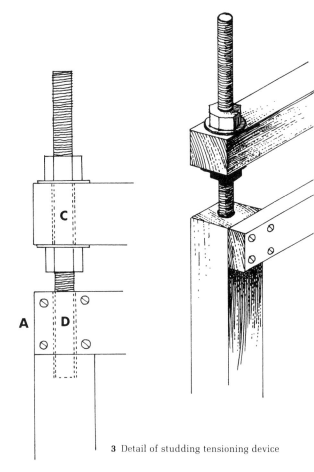

3 Detail of studding tensioning device

studding, does so easily. This additional cross piece is 90 cm × 5 cm × 5 cm (3 ft × 2 in × 2 in). After fixing the studding into hole D, put one nut and washer on each side, fit the cross piece over at C and tighten it at both sides, when it is lying horizontally, with a washer and a nut. This top nut should be loosened when a variation in warp tension is needed, allowing the nut under the cross piece to be raised or lowered, before both are tightened securely.

The loom can be propped up against a wall, or fixed to brackets, about 30 cm (1 ft) away from a wall, or feet 45 cm × 5 cm × 5 cm (1 ft 6 in × 2 in × 2 in) can be screwed to the uprights, as illustrated. The feet can either be screwed to a bench or held by large G clamps, when the loom is in use.

The variable cross piece, at the top of the loom, and the fixed cross piece, at the bottom, can be strengthened by screwing aluminium strips, the full width × 5 cm × 3 mm (× 2 in × $\frac{1}{8}$ in), to either the back or front of the cross pieces, the screws being spaced every 15 cm (6 in).

For a bigger frame loom use wood up to 10 cm × 5 cm (4 in × 2 in) for the two fixed cross pieces, 8 cm × 8 cm (3 in × 3 in) or 10 cm × 8 cm (4 in × 3 in) for the top cross piece, and 10 cm × 8 cm (4 in × 3 in) for the uprights.

The warp

The warp twine used in all the illustrations in this book is 10/6 linen rug warp, used double. If the warp twine is bought in cops, it can be prepared for use double by fixing two upright lengths of dowel, wood or metal, into holes in a shelf (figure 4). If a suitable bobbin is not available, make one from a length of wood 2.5 cm (1 in) thick and 25 cm (10 in) long. Glue and screw two pieces of wood 2.5 cm × 2.5 cm (1 in × 1 in), one at each end (figure 5). A considerable length of double twine, wound round the bobbin, from side to side, is easy to handle when putting on the warp.

Linen is strong, firm, and pleasant to look at during long periods of weaving. It hangs well, and does not stretch easily. A finished tapestry which has a linen warp should not, however, be folded, because linen retains folds. It is easy and convenient to roll it. In fine work, unbleached linen may stain fine yarns, but 2/5s rug yarn is not affected in this way. For these reasons some weavers prefer cotton as a warp material and, as this is a matter of personal preference, the choice can best be made by experimenting with a small tapestry using a linen warp, followed by one using a cotton warp. The recommendation to use double thickness warp, for a coarse tapestry, spacing four ends per 2.5 cm (1 in), comes from a long experience of finger shedding, using a continuous warp. But the decision to use single or double warp twine is also a personal one, and should be made after experimenting with both.

Before putting on the warp, mark off the top and bottom cross pieces on the frame, or loom, using a felt pen, spacing the marks every 6 mm ($\frac{1}{4}$ in), and allowing a margin of 2.5 cm (1 in) or so inside the weaving space on the frame, or loom (figure 6).

Start the warping process by tying the warp twine securely to either the top or bottom cross

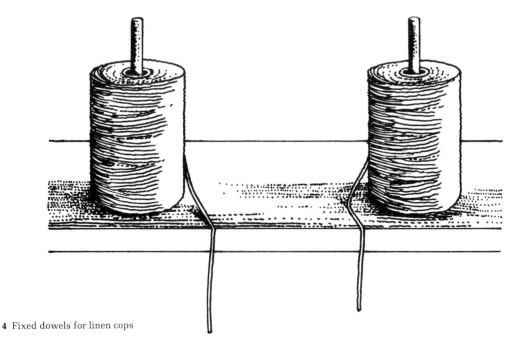

4 Fixed dowels for linen cops

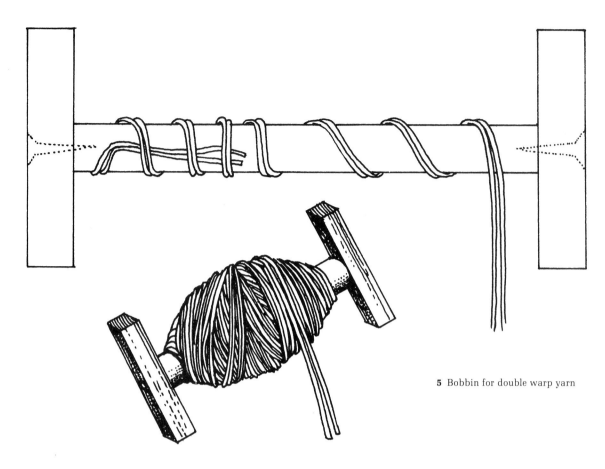

5 Bobbin for double warp yarn

piece, on the left- or right-hand side, or to a nail or screw fixed at the back of the top or bottom cross piece. Carry the warp twine round the loom in a continuous length, spacing it according to the marks, and keep it taut and even. When the required width has been reached, tie round the top or bottom cross piece, or to a nail or screw at the back of the loom. Adjust the tension of the warp if, on testing with the fingers, it is slack in some sections, by starting at one edge, pulling each end or thread down and round. Take up the slack at the bottom until it becomes too long to handle easily, at which point it can be cut and tied firmly under the bottom cross piece. If the frame loom, described earlier, is being used, the top cross piece can be adjusted by tightening, or slackening the nuts. The warp should be tight and, at the same time, easy to raise with the fingers. Practice over a period of time will

decide the degree of tension which is most effective.

Even spacing of the warp can be assisted by twining a fairly thick yarn across the whole warp, just under the top cross piece. The twining is carried out about half way up the warp, and the yarn is pushed up into position afterwards. Attach a length of woollen yarn, which is four times the width of the loom, to one upright on the left or right (figure 7). Carry the twining thread through to the other side of the loom, over and under alternate warp ends, and attach it to the other side of the loom. It helps if a stick slightly longer than the width of the warp and about $20\,mm \times 3\,mm$ ($\frac{3}{4}\,in \times \frac{1}{8}\,in$) is inserted under alternate warp ends across the warp. When this stick is turned on its edge it makes a shed, which facilitates the passing of the twining thread. A finger action, raising alternate warp ends in sequence, achieves the same

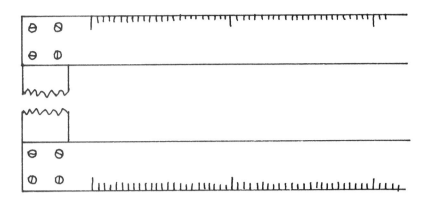

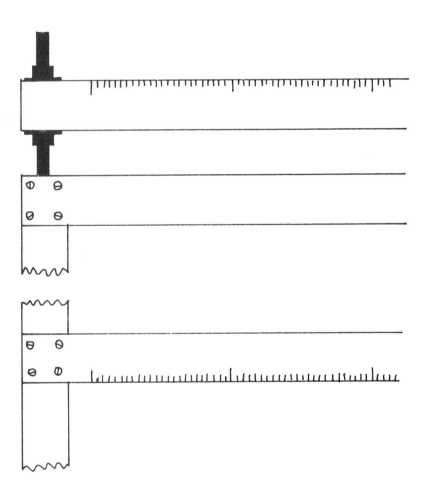

6 Marking the frame for setting the warp

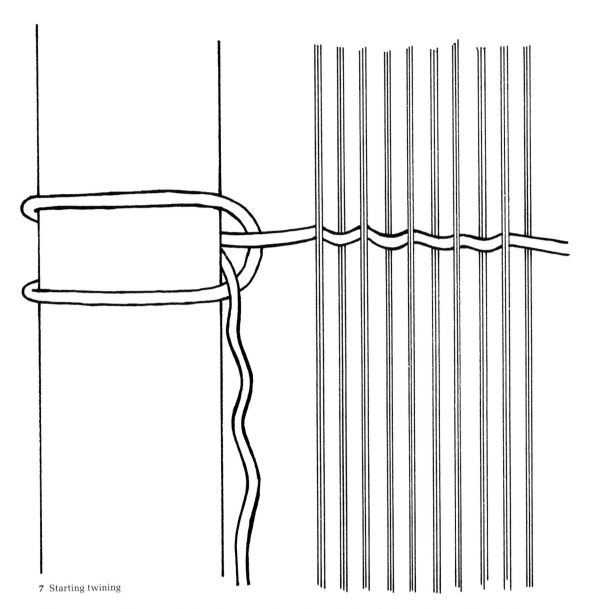

7 Starting twining

result. Now pass the second thread over and under (figure 8) until every warp end is bound and spaced at the correct intervals. Attach both threads to the other side of the loom, after pushing the twining to the top of the loom, where it controls the warp spacing, while allowing maximum length for the warp during the weaving process.

In order to make a firm base for the weaving of the weft, one or two sticks or lengths of cardboard similar to the shed stick, but thinner in the case of cardboard, should be passed through the sheds and pressed to the bottom of the loom. It will have been appreciated already that two sheds are made, the one by raising warp threads or ends 1, 3, 5 and so on in sequence, the other by raising ends 2, 4, 6 and so on. Figure 9 shows part of a frame, in which the warp, the twining and the two lengths of card, or sticks, keep the spacing regular and the base of the tapestry secure. In the diagram the frame and the sticks are not to scale, but the warp, weft and twining are actual size.

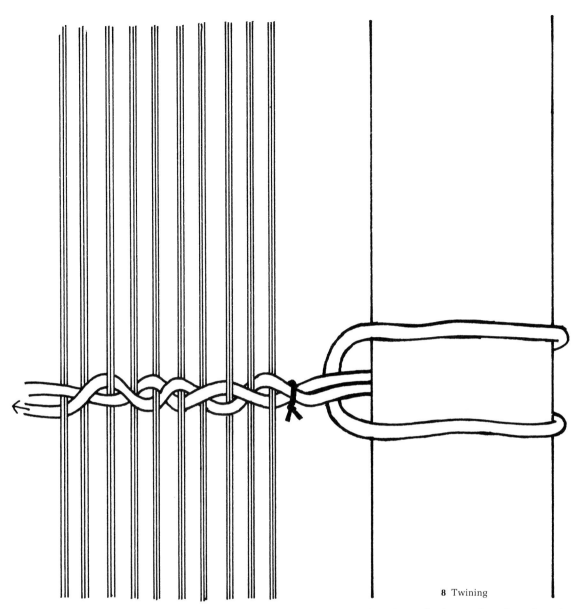

8 Twining

The weft

The woollen yarn recommended is 2/5s rug yarn. Of course, any wool, cotton, linen, silk, or other fibre, can be used, thick or thin, according to the thickness and spacing of the warp and the sort of surface effect which is required. 2/5s yarn will, however, give good results, on a loom set up as described in this chapter. If possible, in the early stages of experiments in tapestry, buy a range of natural colours, from white, through greys, to natural black. Too great a variety is confusing and, unless there is a strong contrary feeling, it is best to start with four tones: white, light grey, middle grey and dark grey or natural black. Figure 10 shows a large sampler, 32 cm × 147 cm (1 ft 1 in × 4 ft 10 in), which was woven on the author's large iron frame loom. A series of experiments in weft patterns were carried out in a random fashion. It is not strictly necessary to weave a sampler, although it is useful for some weavers to do so. The range of weft patterns can be experienced and practised as the need arises, rather than in

17

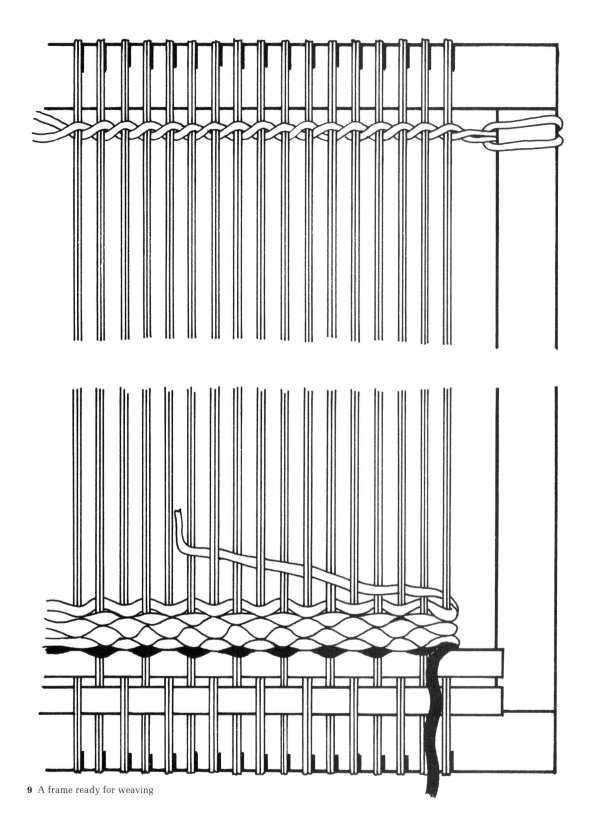

9 A frame ready for weaving

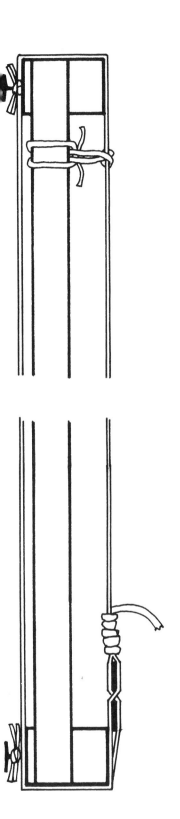

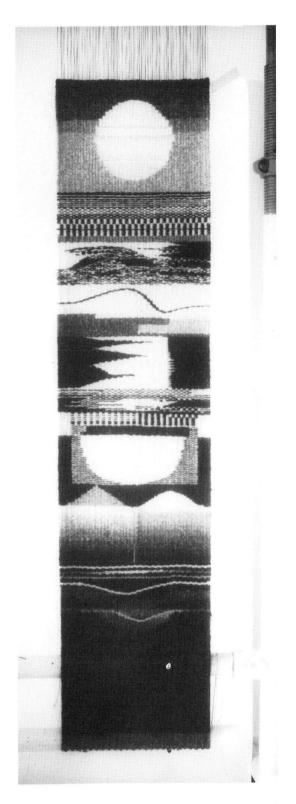

10 Sampler on loom

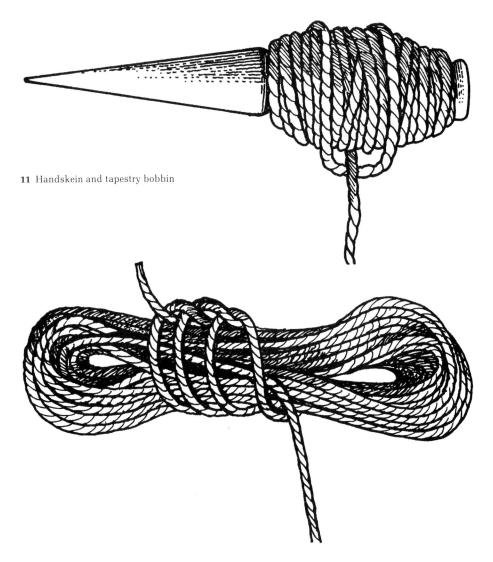

11 Handskein and tapestry bobbin

a complete series as a preliminary to making a tapestry. One weaver may prefer to start a tapestry which is made of simple, clear shapes, consisting mainly of horizontals, diagonals and curves. An understanding of the stepping techniques is the main technical requirement. Another weaver may feel confident only if all the techniques have been experienced. Advice on the making of a sampler and the techniques involved are presented, therefore, either for consumption in one sitting or for reference over a period of time.

To weave a small sampler, 25 cm (10 in) wide, set up a frame, or loom, as previously described. Make a small handskein of wool (also called a dolly, or butterfly, fingerskein or, simply, ball), from about a 200 cm (6–7 ft) length, using black, or white, or one of the greys. Start by winding three times round the thumb, then cross to the little finger, or the index finger, continuing in a figure of eight, until the skein is big enough. End with two or three half-hitches around the middle of the skein.

The yarn can be pulled out from the thumb end. An alternative method, which is less complicated in the making and in use, is to follow the figure of eight around thumb and index finger, and to finish by wrapping several times round the waist of the resulting ball. Although this unrolls itself sometimes in practice, re-

'Scottish landscape', 165cm x 120cm (5ft 5in x 4ft)

'Lake, hills and sea',
90cm x 120cm (3ft x 4ft)

'Village in hills',
135cm x 165cm
(4ft 6in x 5ft 6 in)

rolling is instinctive, and gives occasional and useful pause for viewing the work. Tapestry bobbins can also be helpful. As in the first type of handskein the yarn is looped so that the bobbin hangs, without unrolling itself, when not in use. In figure 11 the bobbin illustrated is about 12 cm (5 in) long. The handskeins are usually about the same length. If they are longer it is difficult to pass them along the warp.

Plain tapestry weave (figure 12) covers the warp, the weft being laid in alternating sheds. Leave about 10 cm (4 in) hanging in front, to be stitched in later. Practise the making of the sheds with the fingers. Hold the ball, or bobbin, in one hand, keeping it secure with the thumb, while the fingers lift alternating warp ends. The second finger and the index finger tend to do the work, while the other two follow along passively. Five or six ends should be raised. As the technique is mastered more are possible, and the speed of the operation also increases. Once the shed has been raised the ball of wool is drawn across, using the other hand, while both hands control the laying in of the weft. The yarn should not be pulled tight, but laid in a loop and pressed down firmly with the fingers, so that it sits nicely, without pulling the warp out of true. It takes some time before there is control over the tension in the weft. The yarn passes round the edge of the warp (the selvedge) and back again. The tension, when properly controlled, ensures that the selvedge is straight as the area of plain weave grows. Measure the width of the sampler every 2 cm ($\frac{3}{4}$ in) to make sure that the weft is neither too tight—which results in waisting—nor too slack. Constant awareness of the importance of weft tension is essential. To change the colour leave about 10 cm (4 in) of the first yarn hanging at the back of the loom. Introduce the new colour by pushing the end of the yarn through the next opening between warp ends, leave it hanging, and proceed. In traditional tapestry weaving the ends of the yarn were left hanging in front, the back of the work becoming the eventual front. There is an obvious choice here. But, in practice, it is convenient to see the work grow up, without confusing bits of yarn hanging

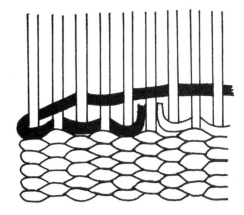

12 Plain tapestry weave

13 Vertical stripes

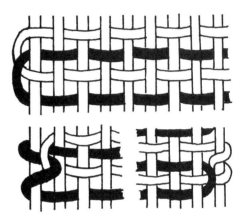

down in front. If the ends of the yarn are about 10 cm (4 in) they can be left hanging, without stitching them in. The subsequent lines of weft pack them down firmly.

Each line of weft yarn is called a pick. Alternating picks of two colours produce vertical stripes, each covered warp end representing one stripe. In figure 13 the second diagram shows how the weft is woven at the selvedges in order to continue the stripes consistently across the warp. To break the sequence of stripes, and to make a fine chequered pattern, change the colour after two or three picks of each colour. Fine horizontal stripes are achieved by weaving two picks of each colour, and then repeating. The correct way to do this is illustrated in figure 14 in the first diagram. Each colour is taken continuously, overlapping at the selvedges. In the second diagram much the same effect is gained by breaking each colour at a different point across the warp each time the colour is changed.

Diagonals and curves are made by weaving steps. The sequence is easy to follow in figure 15. Two picks make one small step in the pattern, the weft yarns approaching each other from each outside, and returning via adjacent warp ends. When packed down this small step produces a very acute angled diagonal. In figure 16 additional picks deepen the step and increase the angle. A step made of more than ten picks is likely to result in a series of slits,

which may not be acceptable in the finished work. Slits can be stitched from the back but, if the steps are too deep, it may be advisable to resort to joining devices, which will be dealt with shortly (figures 23 to 28).

Diagonals which form triangles or lozenges are made by stepping up the outside shapes first (figures 17 and 18). Figure 18 is numbered to show the sequence used to weave triangular shapes. The aim at all times in tapestry weaving is to keep the sheds open, and to avoid overhanging shapes, which enclose sections of the warp in which the fingers cannot open the shed. Figures 19, 20 and 21 apply this principle to circular forms. The weaving sequence should always be strictly adhered to. It must be emphasised, however, that it is not necessary to weave complete shapes. Referring again to

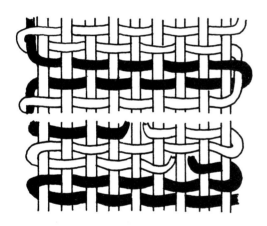

14 Horizontal stripes

15 Weaving steps for diagonals and curves

16 Increasing the angle with bigger steps

17 Triangle or lozenge

figure 18, it is possible to weave about ten picks of the two shapes labelled 1, followed by ten picks of 2, and so on, until the three shapes are complete. Then, ten picks of 3, followed by ten picks each of the two shapes labelled 4, and so on, until all the shapes are finished. Depending on the size of the shapes, the number of picks is variable. A small triangle may be woven in one piece, whereas a large one might be taken in stages. If one shape penetrates too far up the warp, at the expense of its surrounding shapes, there is a danger of getting into trouble with weft tension.

There are times, for example when weaving the upper half of a circle, when it might seem to be necessary to complete the shape before deciding on the treatment of the two adjacent background areas. In spontaneous weaving, when no preliminary designs are being used, this is likely to happen from time to time, because it is easier to visualise a possible colour when a main area is already there. The instincts of the weaver, rather than over cautious considerations of the difficulties of weft tension, should take precedence here. Provided that the open shed principle is understood, and you are prepared to unpick the work if the warp has been pulled in too much, it pays to take some risks in tapestry weaving. Figures 20 and 21 have already been referred to, but a further look at them should be taken, noting that, while triangles have consistent steps, circles and curves are made by increasing, or decreasing, the number of picks in a step as the shape develops.

Traditionally tapestries were made so that the

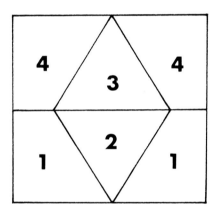

18 Numbered sequence in weaving triangle or lozenge

19 Numbered sequence in weaving a circle

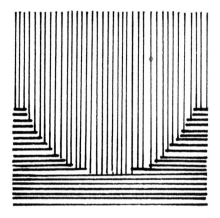

20 Stepping a curve

21 Increasing steps in a curve

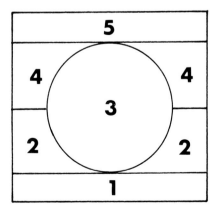

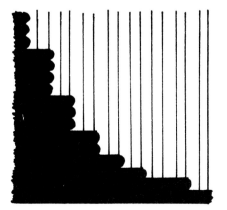

23

weft would hang vertically. It was, therefore, necessary to set the design sideways on the warp. The natural action of laying in the weft always resulted in an emphasis on the horizontal, which became the vertical, once the tapestry was cut off the loom, and made ready for hanging. Large and long tapestries, with many vertical figures, were more easily woven on looms which were a little wider than the required height of the tapestry. A piece 900 cm long × 300 cm high (30 ft × 10 ft) could be woven on a loom which was a little wider than 30 cm (10 ft). But there were additional advantages. For example, the tonal contrasts in faces were more effective with the light falling on a vertical weft. Buildings, tree trunks, flowers, legs and costumes tend to have a vertical emphasis. But often the weight of the tapestry, over the years, opened up the slits, which were vertical on the loom but horizontal in the finished work. So there were some disadvantages. It is difficult for an individual, contemporary weaver, to build up the work sideways without resorting to detailed preliminary designs. It is also strenuous, if the head has to be bent over constantly, to see how the design is progressing. Figure 22, a small tapestry, 'Hill town', was woven with the left side at the bottom of the loom. When hung sideways, the resulting verticals give the work its character. It would have been difficult, although not impossible, to weave this piece if the warp was meant to hang vertically, like all the other tapestries in this book.

There are a number of joining methods for vertical divisions in tapestries where the weft remains horizontal (see figures 23 to 28). If a vertical slit is not acceptable, because it would weaken the tapestry, try one of the following joining methods which, it will be assumed, are being experimented with in black and white woollen yarns.

Figure 23. Bring each pick of weft towards the warp end, which marks the vertical division; go round it, and return along the next shed. In the second drawing in figure 23 it is made clear that this method produces a certain filling up along the warp end and, therefore, a

22 *Opposite:* Tapestry: 'Hill town'. 104 cm × 83 cm (3 ft 5 in × 2 ft 9 in)

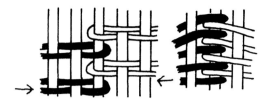

23 Avoiding vertical slits

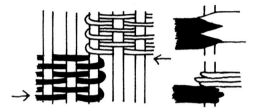

24 Avoiding vertical slits

25 Avoiding vertical slits

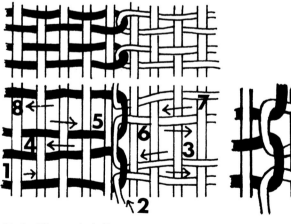

26 Avoiding vertical slits

27 Avoiding vertical slits

28 A vertical: crossing into adjacent colour area

slight bulge in the tapestry. For a short vertical this is all right, but a long vertical can look clumsy.

Figure 24. A group of three black returns around the dividing warp end, followed by three white returns, results in an attractive serrated appearance up the vertical. There is again, however, the problem of the thickening warp end.

Figure 25 is similar to figure 23, but the picks are balanced on each side of the vertical by additional returns to black and white, around each immediately adjacent warp end, to the right and to the left.

Figure 26 makes the vertical in the space between the warp ends. This works out easily if the numbered sequence is followed carefully. Watch the tension where the black and white yarns hook round each other.

Figure 27 keeps to the total slit so far as the main weft yarns are concerned. But an additional very thin yarn of wool, cotton, linen, or an artificial fibre is laid in short lengths across about eight warp ends, and left with the weft ends hanging down the back. This additional yarn is laid in every four picks (two returns). The idea is to make an invisible join at regular intervals.

Figure 28 affects the tone of the white area and makes it grey. The black yarn is taken across the white shape, after each return. This results in horizontal stripes. Try this and then make two or more returns (four or more picks) before taking several picks across the white area. The white must, of course, be filled up as the work proceeds in order to keep a balance. When using this method be careful not to give sideways pull to the warp ends which mark the slit.

Undulating lines in a design are dealt with in figure 29. The black area represents a curve which must be woven carefully before laying in the line. The line can be two or up to six picks in thickness. It can travel over steps of two or four picks (one or two returns round a warp end). When the angle is steeper the weft should be taken round the warp ends, corresponding with the number of picks in a step, so that the line

itself becomes stepped. In practice it becomes obvious that this is necessary. Experiment with a few lines of different and varying thickness, along gentle and steep curves. Only when the line has been laid in can the next shapes above be filled in. In doing so, repeat the steps of the original curve. This is made clear in the diagram. There are, sometimes, variations in the sheds when a number of colours are involved. One pick of the weft sits easily in its shed, on one side of a curve, above a line. And then, as the colour change is passed over, the shed, along which the weft is travelling, is found to be filled. Usually, an additional length of yarn can be laid in to balance the sheds and to bring the pick in front of the correct warp ends. It soon becomes a habit when dealing with a series of small shapes to glance along the warp so that one can see from which direction the next colour must come, in order to cross alternating warp ends, in a consistent shed.

The structure in figure 30 can be used for short vertical lines. In the diagram, the short vertical is leading into a curve, but it might be the trunk of a tree or a free-standing short line in a pattern. When preparing the tapestry for hanging the back of the slits must be stitched, and the end of the weft yarn threaded down an adjacent warp end, in order to anchor it.

Figures 31 and 32 illustrate some of the ways of varying visual textures. Short lengths of single and double yarns are laid in. The weft ends hang down the back. In a heavily textured area a thick pile can build up rapidly at the back of the tapestry. If the hanging weft ends are kept to about 8 cm (3 in) in length they usually hang flat later, against the wall. Two thicknesses of yarn, in different colours, can be twisted to vary the texture further. Try out one of these figures, but when the principle is clear, make individual variations and experiments. This type of texturing can easily be over-used. It is particularly tempting to use it when drawings or paintings are being closely imitated (not a good idea anyway). The effect is rather like a currant bun, spotty and boring, in large lumps. Used in small doses with the other woven structures and areas of plain weave it can be very pleasant to look at.

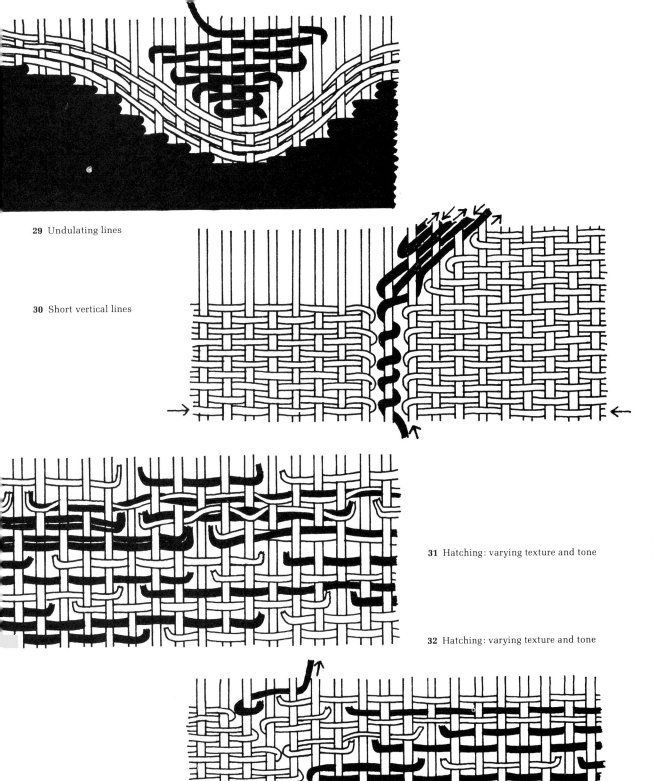

29 Undulating lines

30 Short vertical lines

31 Hatching: varying texture and tone

32 Hatching: varying texture and tone

33 Detail from tapestry: 'Grey tarn'

34 *Opposite:* A circle from a sampler

Eight photographs of details of tapestries (figures 33–40) summarise the weft structures. In the middle section of the circle in figure 33, the structure of figure 28 is used extensively. The background colour comes across the slit, into the circle, and then goes back into the background. The steep step of the circle is built up securely.

The steps in the middle areas of the small circle in figure 34 are joined by the method described in figure 23. The horizontal and vertical stripes, below the circle, are the result of figures 13 and 14.

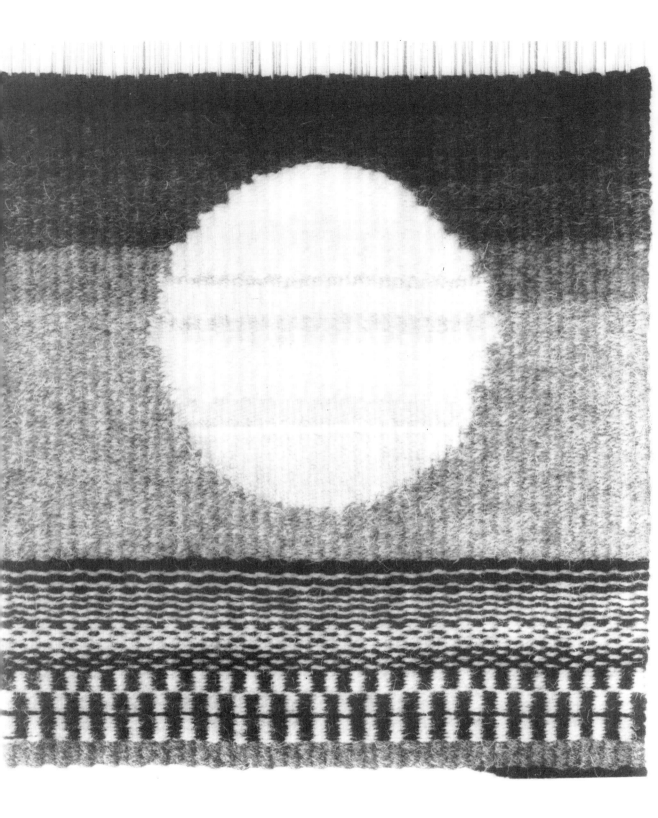

29

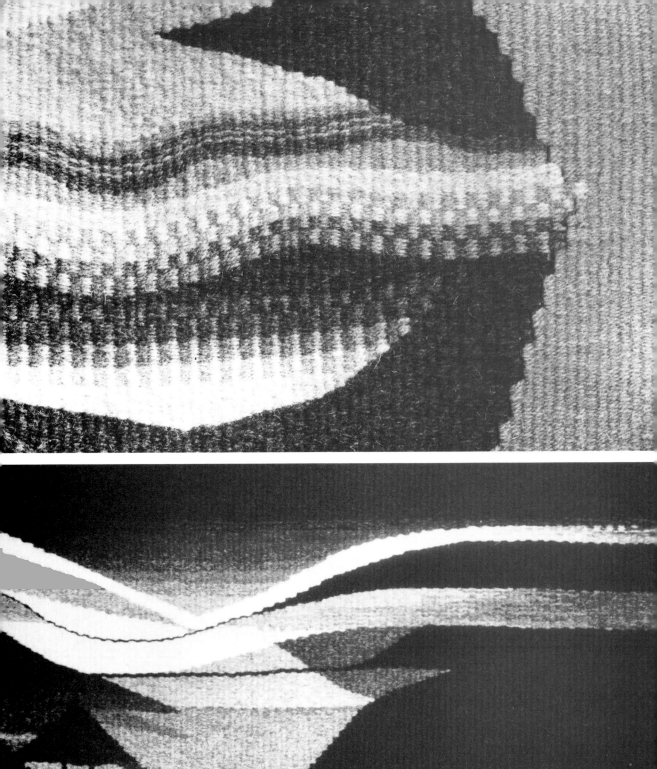

35 *Opposite, above:* Detail from tapestry: 'Black fells'

36 *Opposite, below:* Detail from tapestry: 'Cumbrian land-scape'

37 *Above:* Detail from tapestry: 'Roads into a village'

Figure 35 combines the vertical stripe structure of figure 13 with the undulating lines of figure 29, with frequent colour changes.

In figure 36, figures 15 and 16 are used, above the single line of figure 30. The lines of varying thickness (figure 29) are an important part of this design.

Apart from other obvious weaves, the central area of figure 37 has colour and tonal changes based on figures 15, 16 and 17.

The upper left textured area of figure 38 combines figures 13 and 14 with figures 31 and 32.

Apart from single undulating lines and verticals, all the weft structures described are used in figures 39 and 40.

Colour and tonal variations can transform a simple weft structure. Those who like to experiment on small pieces may find the following interesting:

1 Make a small piece, using figures 12, 13 and 14 only, in black and white, in imaginative combinations.

2 Using the same three weft structures, take a light tone of a colour, and a slightly darker tone of the same, or a similar, colour. Weave a small tapestry.

38 *Opposite, above:* Detail from tapestry: 'Black fells'

39 *Opposite, below:* Detail from tapestry: 'Sea and islands'

40 *Above:* Detail from tapestry: 'Sea and islands'

3 Use several tones of two contrasting colours. The contrasting, or opposite, colours, are green/red, yellow/violet, or orange/blue.

4 Weave a small panel, using a series of finely graded tones of a colour, or of colours, limiting the structure to plain tapestry weave (figure 12). Do not attempt to use texture where the tone changes, but change the colour along one pick by breaking the yarn and allowing it to hang down the back at the break point. Introduce the new tone in the next space along, between warp ends.

Warp and weft structure: some alternatives

What follows, in this section, is largely for those who wish to use a finer warp. Making the sheds with the fingers (finger shedding) is a fairly quick method of laying in the weft when the warp spacing is four double ends per 2.5 cm (1 in). A reminder of the finger shedding technique will be appropriate, before the use of

41 Finger shedding with a handskein

42 Finger shedding with a handskein

leashes is explained.

Figures 41 to 46 show the passage of a handskein of weft yarn through the sheds. The index finger (figure 41), with the thumb, makes a temporary holding device for the yarn after

it has opened the shed. The other fingers open up the shed, and the handskein is transferred to the other hand (figures 42, 43, 44). After the pick has been pressed down, the hand opens up the next shed (figure 45), and the wool is passed to it by the other hand. In the photographs it will be observed that the leading hand is the left one. This is a variable, and the hand which takes the lead naturally is the one to rely on.

43 Finger shedding with a handskein

44 Finger shedding with a handskein

There is no rule about this. Tapestry weaving is slow, but an experienced weaver, using this technique, can on average weave about 30 cm square (1 ft square) in a reasonable working day.

45 Finger shedding with a handskein

46 Finger shedding with a handskein

The procedure with bobbins is much the same (figures 47 to 51). In figure 48, however, string loops, or leashes, are used to open the shed. A shed stick which is higher up the warp, opens the second shed. In figure 52, photographed from below, the shed stick is on its side, lifting the alternate warp ends, unhindered by the leashes which are hanging slack round the warp ends at the back of the shed.

47 and 48 Finger shedding with a bobbin

The bar, to which the leashes are attached, is fixed at a point in front of the loom. Before describing the leashes and leash bar an intermediate technique should be referred to.

Instead of four double warp ends per 2.5 cm (1 in), the warp ends can be used singly, spacing

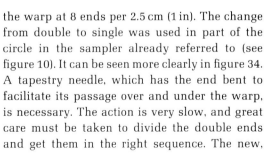

the warp at 8 ends per 2.5 cm (1 in). The change from double to single was used in part of the circle in the sampler already referred to (see figure 10). It can be seen more clearly in figure 34. A tapestry needle, which has the end bent to facilitate its passage over and under the warp, is necessary. The action is very slow, and great care must be taken to divide the double ends and get them in the right sequence. The new,

49 Finger shedding with a bobbin

50 Finger shedding with a bobbin

51 *Opposite, left:* Finger shedding with a bobbin

52 *Opposite, right:* Using a shed stick and leashes

finer, weave packs easily into the coarser weave. The weft should never be beaten down too hard. The packing down should only be firm enough to cover the warp, and to keep it covered. Normally the weight of the hand is sufficient. Sometimes the end of a bobbin can be used for small shapes, when the point presses down the weft more easily.

If the whole warp is spaced at 6 or 8 ends per 2.5 cm (1 in) it is essential to use a shed stick and leashes for making the shed. To make leashes, cut 50 cm (1 ft 8 in) lengths of cotton or linen thread. Place a stick across the warp under alternating warp ends. Loop each leash round the warp ends which lie on top of this stick. Fix a 2.5 cm or 4 cm (1 in or 1½ in) dowel rod to two large G-clamps, at each side of the loom (figure 53), so that it is out in front of the loom and

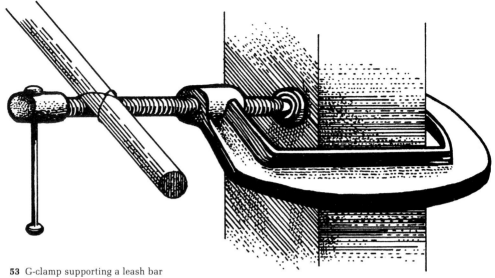

53 G-clamp supporting a leash bar

54 Tying a leash

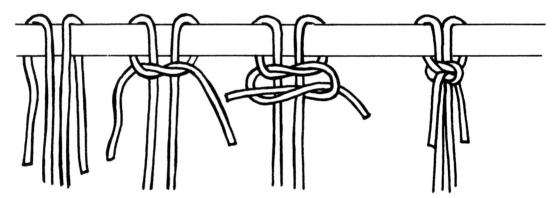

above the level at which the leashes are looped around the warp ends. Tie the leashes individually, to the leash bar by taking both ends of the leash over and round the bar, and then forward to be knotted as in figure 54. Because of the G-clamps the bar can be moved up the loom as the weaving progresses.

Place a shed stick, about 2 cm × 2 cm, or 2.5 cm × 1.5 cm ($\frac{3}{4}$ in × $\frac{3}{4}$ in or 1 in × $\frac{1}{2}$ in), across the loom, under the alternate warp ends which were not taken up by the leashes. This shed stick must be higher than the leashes in order to make the second shed possible. To make the first shed pull a group of five or so leashes forward, and then pass the fingers through. Continue like this across the warp. The second shed is per-

manently there if a 2 cm × 2 cm stick is in use, but it can be made more emphatic if the 2.5 cm × 1.5 cm stick is turned on its edge. Figure 55 shows part of a frame loom, set up with warp, leashes, shed stick, leash bar and the additional lower stick; the lower stick can be removed, finally, as its only function was to mark the warp ends round which the leashes were to go. Figures 56 and 57 illustrate the two sheds. In figure 56 a shed stick is turned on its edge.

This system is appropriate for all finer warps. It is wise to double check that the leashes are round alternating ends across the whole warp, in the right sequence, before tying them to the leash bar.

40

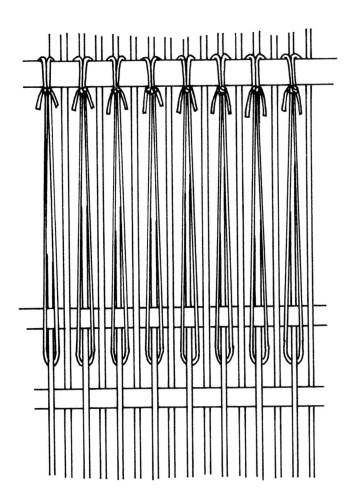

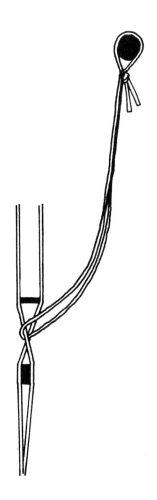

55 Leashes, shed stick and leash bar in position

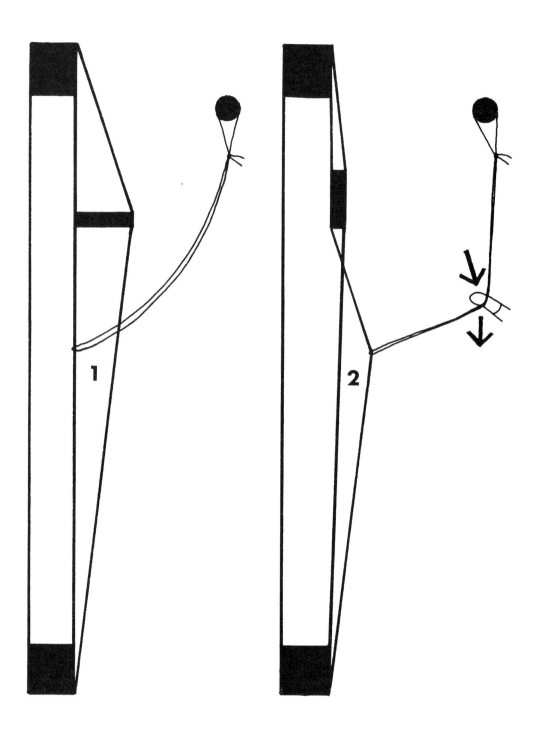

56 First shed

57 Second shed

Dyeing

Wool can be bought ready dyed in a range of colours, some of which are specially prepared for the tapestry weaver. Some weavers make up colours in a range of shades and tones by buying thin single colours in yarn, direct from the woollen mills, on cones or cylinders (pirns). Several colours are then laid or twisted together from these cones to make up a yarn of a suitable thickness. Subtle variations are possible by the addition or subtraction of a single colour from a group of such yarns. The mixed yarns can be prepared well ahead, so that a complete range is always available for choice.

For those who would like to have some experience of dyeing, one method of dyeing natural yarn will be described in this section. Hot water dyes are used (Dylon). Small tins, which dye 250 g ($\frac{1}{2}$ lb) of wool, are convenient, but bottles, from which a measured portion can be taken, might be preferred.

Prepare the wool in 250 g ($\frac{1}{2}$ lb), or in 50 g (2 oz) or 25 g (1 oz) hanks to make up 250 g ($\frac{1}{2}$ lb). Tie three short lengths of string loosely round the yarn (see figure 58), and one longer length to hang over the edge of the dye bath but well clear of the heat source (see figure 59).

Wash and rinse, or wet the wool thoroughly in warm water. Prepare the dye, as instructed. Always follow the maker's instructions care-

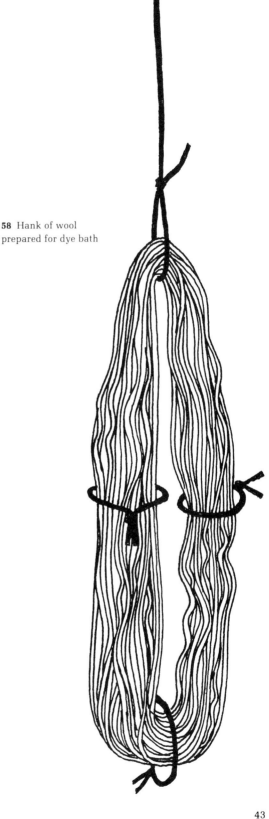

58 Hank of wool prepared for dye bath

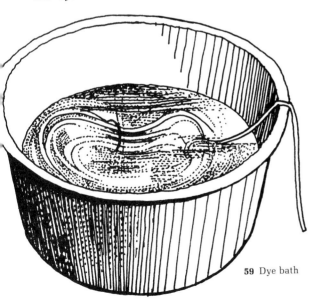

59 Dye bath

43

fully. Into a stainless steel bucket, or bowl, put enough warm water to cover the wool, so that it moves around easily; before putting the wool into the bath add the dye and mix well. Remember to add salt (in the case of Dylon, for example). Use a wooden spoon or stick to mix, stir and hold up the wool, or to press it down. Hold the wool in a loose ball and immerse quickly, in one smooth, unhurried movement. Press the wool down, so that all parts take up the dye easily and evenly, and then stir the bath a little. Heat the bath to the required temperature (boiling, in the case of Dylon), covering with a lid, if necessary, and simmer to keep at the required temperature for the correct length of time.

The wool can cool in the bath or be lifted out and allowed to cool outside the bath, before rinsing with warm water until traces of colour are not visible in the rinsing water. If it is allowed to cool outside the bath, squeeze out excess dye and move the hank before rinsing so that any other excess dye does not settle in one group of fibres. Allow the wool to dry naturally. A spin dry removes much of the water, and the wool can then be hung out to dry thoroughly. It is obvious that the amount of wool which it is possible to dye in one session depends on the capacity of the bath and the source of heating. On an ordinary kitchen gas ring or hot plate a maximum load of 750 g (1½ lb) is recommended. The amount will soon become clear after a few experiments. Often 250 g (½ lb) is enough to deal with effectively. If there is unevenness in the dyeing, the cause can be poor washing or wetting, in which case a wetting agent may be used; or attempting to dye too large a quantity of wool in one bath. If you hesitate and fumble, the first half of a hank can take up too much dye, particularly if the wool is not stirred and moved through the bath.

One of the advantages of using natural wools, in a range of white to dark grey, is that the same colour of dye will produce a range of tones of each colour. For example, prepare four 50 g (2 oz) hanks in white, and three tones of grey. Join the long strings, after tying the hanks, by tying them at the top, so that they can be handled in one hank, as it were (see figure 60). The dyeing proceeds as above. Do not allow one hank to enter the bath later than another, to avoid variation in the take-up of the dye. The use of this tonal-range system results in a harmonious collection of tones and colours.

An accurate record of each dyeing session will save time and uncertainty in subsequent sessions. This can be done in several ways. Three ways are illustrated in figures 61, 62 and 63, one in the form of a book, the others on cards. The book has the advantage that additional notes can be entered; the cards are useful if clients are involved, and a range of colours are being sent for approval. In figure 61, a piece of tape holds the wool in position, but it could be stuck with an adhesive on the back of the wool, for a neater appearance. In figure 62, wool is wound round one piece of card. It is tied at the back and then stuck down on a bigger piece of card, on which notes are written. This method enables the colour to be seen in a 3 cm to 5 cm (1 in to 2 in) square. It is easier to judge it against other colours. Figure 63 is, perhaps, the quickest method. It can also be hung in long strips on a studio wall board for quick reference.

Storing wool
The best way to store wool is loosely, in hanks, on slatted shelves allowing for free movement of air. The wool should be shaken and moved occasionally, not left for indefinite periods, piled in corners, or enclosed for a long time in plastic bags.

Mothproofing
Finished work can be sprayed with chemicals, prepared in pressurised containers. These are effective for about three to six months. Moth crystals or balls can be kept on the top shelves, where wool is being stored. Some wool can be bought with a mothproof finish. Normally there is no need to worry much about hangings in the sort of tough woollen yarns recommended, when they are in position on the wall, but they should be vacuumed, shaken lightly and inspected from time to time, back and front and,

'Sand hills and sea', 180cm x 120cm (6ft x 4ft)

'Landscape by a lake',
150cm x 180cm (5ft x 6ft)
Courtaulds Ltd

'Towards the sea',
150cm x 170cm
(4ft 11in x 5ft 7in)

60 Hanks in four tones prepared for dye bath

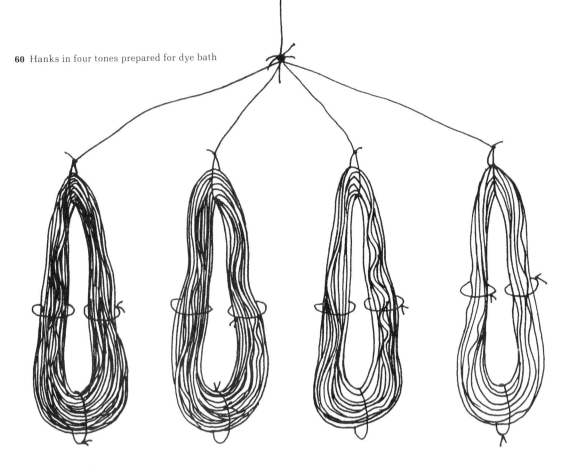

61 A record of dyeing

Date	Dye	Notes	Colour
1/1/83	Coffee on white wool	Craftsman's mark 2/5 Rug yarn	
2/1/83	Coffee as light grey wool	Craftsman's mark 2/5 Rug yarn	

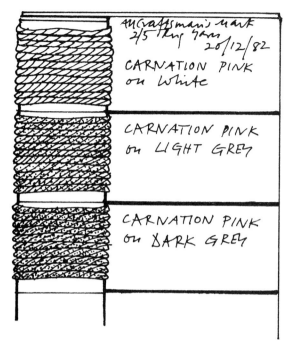

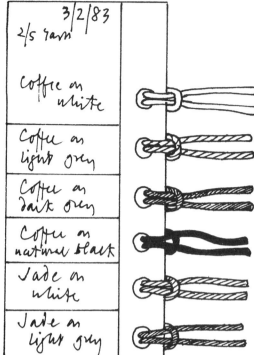

The Craftsman's mark
2/5 Rug yarn
20/12/82

CARNATION PINK on White

CARNATION PINK on LIGHT GREY

CARNATION PINK on DARK GREY

3/2/83
2/5 yarn

Coffee on white

Coffee on light grey

Coffee on dark grey

Coffee on natural black

Jade on white

Jade on light grey

62 A record of dyeing   **63** A record of dyeing

of course, hung out of direct sun light. Moth-proofing, if it is to be permanent, should be carried out at the time of dyeing the wool. There are chemicals which are added in small quantities to the dye bath, but it is sometimes difficult to obtain these in small containers. Enquiries can be made to the Dyestuffs Divisions of chemical industries, or to woollen mills or carpet factories. But it should be realised that these chemicals are supplied to carpet manufacturers in 60 kg drums, and are not available through retail outlets (example: EULAN WA New, a mothproofing chemical made by Bayer UK Limited). Unless there is a specific need to mothproof, wool can be used and dyed as supplied by the spinners.

2 DRAWING AND PAINTING

Basic equipment and materials

Drawing
B and 2B pencils
white, grey and brown artists' pastels
A10 size, good quality smooth white paper
a pen: felt, fibre, giving a good black line;
  Rotring 2000 Isograph 0.50 mm

Painting
two water colour brushes, numbers 6 and 10;
  a one-stroke 2.5 cm ($\frac{1}{2}$ in) brush
a small box of artists' water colours (see
  Experiment 23)
OR pots or tubes of artists' gouache colours
the best smooth watercolour paper which
  you can afford
OR, for gouache, a good quality smooth
  cartridge paper
gummed paper roll, 2.5 cm to 5 cm (1 in to 2 in)
a waterpot
a drawing board (smooth plywood about
  60 cm × 45 cm, 2 ft × 1 ft 6 in, is suitable)

Technique, in drawing and painting, is dependent on the use of the eyes, as well as on the use of tools. Seeing is always a selective process. Walking down a street, for example, one person sees mainly car registration numbers, another trees or buildings, and another people's faces or figures, and so on. Someone who is drawing is even more selective, in responding to colours, to tones of dark and light, to the shapes left between familiar objects, to relationships between shapes, their ambiguity, the way they trigger off the memory of other things. Some artists have selected to a point where only the essence of a visual experience remains. The rhythm of seen things, the kaleidoscope of light and movement, have motivated many painters. What we see is sometimes heightened too by the experience of other arts. Those who can draw will have no difficulty in accepting all this. For those who feel that they cannot draw there are difficulties, both in seeing and in using pencil, pen, or brush. But the difficulties are relatively easy to overcome if the subject is approached with the knowledge and the conviction that it is easy to make a start, after which development, quite naturally, takes time, but will be steady and absorbing. The object is not necessarily to become a brilliant draughtsman, but to be able to put things down on paper, and to extend and enrich the experience of seeing in such a way that ideas for drawings, or paintings, or tapestries are your own rather than someone elses's.

The following experiments are designed to give confidence to those who have little experience of drawing. For the most part they are not illustrated, because illustrations would influence the results and there would be a tendency to copy the illustrations.

Drawing

Experiment 1

Place a small, rectangular loaf of bread in front of you, sideways on. Within a plain postcard, or a piece of card, or stiff paper, cut out a rectangle, 7 cm × 5 cm ($2\frac{3}{4}$ in × 2 in). Hold the card in front of you. Cover, or close, one eye, and look at the loaf through the cut-out rectangle. Move the card near to the loaf, so that it almost fills the rectangle. Then move it nearer to your eye, until the loaf becomes small in relation to the rectangle. Move it again and choose a point at which the loaf sits comfortably in the rectangle. On a sheet of paper, draw a rectangle, 14 cm × 10 cm, or 21 cm × 15 cm ($5\frac{1}{2}$ in × 4 in, or $8\frac{1}{4}$ in × 6 in) and, using a strong, bold line (unless you have a strong preference for a delicate, fine line) draw the outline of the loaf as it sits in the 'viewfinder' or cut-out rectangle. You might like to observe the shape left between the edge of the loaf and the side of the viewfinder. This is a back-door method of observing and drawing the loaf, and it might be easier than observing and drawing the loaf itself. But do not regard this as a regular method. Number this drawing 1 and put it to one side.

Experiment 2

Cut one slice from one end of the loaf and lean it against the cut end at an angle of about 60°. Use the viewfinder again, and view the loaf sideways on until part of the uncut end is not visible but the rest, including the slice, nearly fills the viewfinder. Avoid a three-quarter angled view, as this complicates the angles too much at this stage. Look especially at the space between the slice and the cut end and draw this first, with a firm line. Complete the rest of the slice and the visible part of the loaf. Do not worry, or start rubbing out, if you need to distort the proportions in order to get the rest in. Try a second drawing if necessary. This experiment, and others which follow, are meant to be made inside correctly drawn rectangles on the paper. It will be useful to number each drawing, or to date it, so that you can look back over your progress.

Experiment 3

Toast the cut slice until it is nicely browned. Turn the loaf so that the cut end almost faces you. Lean the toasted slice against the cut end of the loaf. Use the viewfinder until the toasted slice and the end of the loaf nearly fill the rectangle, giving a good view of the slice and a partial view of the cut end. Draw this in outline. Then, using diagonal shading, shade the toasted slice all over. Continue with the diagonal shading, but vary it to indicate variations in the toasting.

Experiment 4

Cut a second slice from the loaf. Spread butter or margarine on the toasted slice, but not quite to the edge, allowing some of the darker toast to show fairly generously. Spread butter or margarine on the second, untoasted slice, followed by a dark jam, again leaving a generous surround of light-coloured bread. Lay the slices side by side, with a very small space between them. Look at both, from above, through the viewfinder. Draw the outlines of the slices and the areas taken up by butter and jam. Shade, using diagonal shading, varying the weight (tone), according to the lightness or darkness of different areas.

Experiment 5

Take the remainder of the loaf, having disposed of the two slices. Repeat Experiment 1, allowing the loaf to fill the rectangle comfortably. Draw in outline and then, using diagonal shading, fill in the large areas of tone first, starting with a light weight and increasingly darkening the shading, Do not try to include every small variation. Aim for a generous treatment which brings the loaf slowly to life on your paper.

Now put all the loaf drawings side by side, so that it can be demonstrated that progress has been made from a simple outline to more complex statements in line and tone.

Experiment 6

Take a large bowl, invert it, and put it on a small, plain towel which lies flat on the table. Place a smaller bowl, also inverted, towards the left and in front of the larger bowl. Arrange a few folds, running left to right, in the towel, in the area in front of the bowls. Ignore the ellipses on the bases of the bowls and, after using the viewfinder, make a simple drawing of the curves of the bowls and the folds. Use a strong outline, bold, or delicate, according to your feelings about it. It is important here to make a choice, bearing in mind only that the line should not look indecisive. There is no need to draw the sides, or the front edge, of the towel, but the back can be indicated, as a division between foreground and background. This may have the effect of turning the objects into a landscape. With a grey, or brown pastel, and a white pastel, shade the background area and the two bowls, rubbing the pastel with the fingers, or with one finger, after shading in the shapes. Fill each shape completely, and vary the tone by adding more white, brown, or grey.

Experiment 7

Look at the drawing completed in Experiment 6 critically, and ask if the shapes balance comfortably within the rectangle. It might help to use the viewfinder on the drawing itself, cutting down the surrounding areas, or the shapes of the bowls. Try now a second drawing, as in 6, but different from it, not only in the shapes, but also in the relationship of the tones.

Experiment 8

Arrange two cushions, which are simply designed, plain, or patterned, one partially covering the other. Using the viewfinder, either vertically, or horizontally, select a position in which one or two corners of the cushions are cut out. Try out various angles until you produce a satisfactory balance of shapes. Draw the main outlines of the cushions, followed by any large shapes in the pattern (if any). Give consideration to the background shapes, which should interest you as much as the shapes of the cushions. Shade with pencil or pastel any shapes which are darker than the lightest parts. These can remain white.

Experiment 9

Examine the furnishings in your room, using the viewfinder to select close-ups of parts of things. Look for relationships between those parts and parts of other things, and also to the background of walls and floor. Spend some time doing this. Make a series of fairly quick drawings, using line only, in the usual rectangles on your paper. Do not hesitate to leave out small details, or to alter shapes slightly if, by doing so, you improve the individual shapes, or the arrangement of parts of the drawing. Choose one of the line drawings, and develop it further, by the addition of tones, working from light to dark.

Experiment 10

Put about three flowers in a vase, so that the heads are close together. Imagine that you are using the viewfinder, by projecting a rectangle, mentally, round the flowers. If you experience difficulties doing this, do not feel obliged to pursue the idea; use the real viewfinder. Draw the flowers, or part of them, starting with the general shapes and progressing slowly to the smallest. This will allow you to be satisfied with the main design before proceeding to the details. Pay attention to the background areas, which are as important as the flowers. Shade, working from large to small shapes, bearing in mind that the shapes of areas of tone are as significant as the shapes of the flowers and the background.

Experiment 11

Choose a bush, or a bushy tree, or a bushy indoor plant. Ignore the pot, in the case of the indoor plant. Start by shading lightly in pencil the area inside a rectangle on the drawing paper which is to be occupied by the bush. Keep the shading close in texture. If it helps to bind it into a mass, rub it with a finger. Look at the bush with half closed eyes, from time to time, so that details are lost and the simple shapes of darks and lights are appreciated. Continue to add shading, representing leaves, or groups of leaves, with increasingly dark tones. Use a line only where you can see a clear line.

Repeat the experiment using pastel instead of pencil. Repeat again, using a pen, to see if the linear shading, which is forced on to you by the point of a pen, appeals to you. Shading can be in all directions, unless it destroys the unity of the drawing. It may be preferable to slope it in one direction only. Note that in diagonal shading right-handed draughtsmen slope from right to left, and left-handed from left to right. In this drawing leave the background and foreground white, unless there seems to be a good reason for developing those parts.

Experiment 12
Look at your face in a mirror, preferably a rectangular one which makes it possible for you to position yourself so that the shapes left between your head and the edges of the mirror are interesting. Use either pencil, pastel, or pen throughout. Draw, either by using line only, or

shading only, at the start. Concentrate on the large shapes and work towards the smaller ones, and concentrate initially on the larger tones, followed by the small areas of tone. The proportion of the features might cause some problems, because a face will seem, suddenly, to be much more difficult than the objects in previous experiments. Its flexibility, the fact that it looks at you and changes moods quickly, may cause you to concentrate more on expression and likeness than on form. You should think only of the shapes. Two simple devices can be of assistance:

1 Along the side of the viewfinder make clear marks, dividing one edge into centimetres or

64 Viewfinder with cotton grid divisions

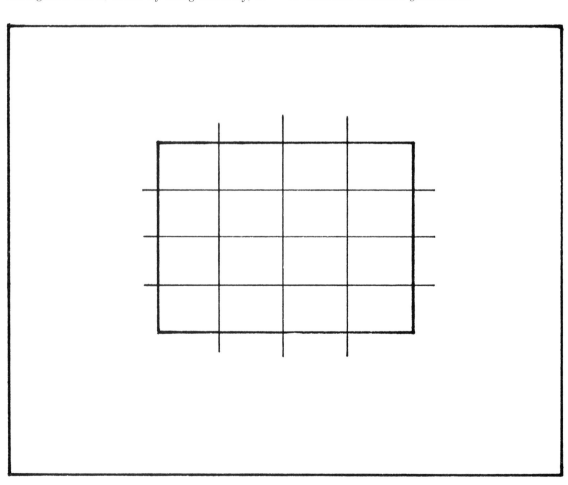

inches and divisions of inches. Hold this up and, keeping a constant distance, measure off the divisions against nose, eyes, mouth, forehead and so on. Make a series of marks on your paper plotting these divisions. Holding up a pencil and running the thumb up and down, using one section as a measuring device, can achieve the same end.

2 Mark off all the edges of the viewfinder, dividing the opening into halves and quarters. Glue some cotton thread across in both directions, making the opening into a grid (figure 64). If the rectangle in which you are to make the drawing has the same proportions as the viewfinder, the drawing area can be divided very lightly into halves and quarters. The head can then be plotted accurately by holding up the viewfinder. If this seems to be too mechanical, do not use it. But if it is used in the early stages of the drawing as an aid to making visual judgements about the proportions of the object it can leave you free, in the later stages, to draw freely and with increasing confidence.

Repeat the experiment, lighting your head from one side with a strong light. Concentrate on light and dark shapes, rather than on the features, allowing the eyes, nose and mouth to emerge as incidentals in the lighting scheme.

Experiment 13
Look at yourself, full figure, in a mirror. If you are wearing clothes keep them simple, not disguising the figure with voluminous folds or trivial patterns. If possible, get someone to pose for you, bearing in mind that it is a strenuous occupation and that it is difficult to keep a pose for any length of time. Keep the pose simple, perhaps seated, with arms loosely to the sides or on the lap; legs almost together. Draw, nearly filling the rectangle, in line, using pencil, pastel, or pen. Devices for measuring, as in Experiment 12, can be used, but not for the first drawing. In the first drawing make a number of flowing lines which represent the figure, without worrying too much about proportions. Plot the proportions in a second drawing, but do both drawings fairly quickly.

Do several drawings, changing the pose and varying the lighting: above, below, to the side, front, back only.

Experiment 14
Select a landscape, seascape, or townscape. Use an actual view, and not a photograph of a view. If the experiments so far have been carried through in sequence, you are now able to see objects, or parts of objects, in depth, in relation to each other, and to represent them on a flat surface. In a landscape the parts are further away from each other than in Experiments 1 to 13, but the principle of relationships remains the same as the shapes are assembled on your drawing paper. For this drawing use a viewfinder and reduce the shapes to a few only, confining them to a sparse arrangement of horizontal, vertical, diagonal and undulating forms in which there are few details. Shade so that the shapes are clearly contrasted, using a range of tones, and keeping the shading mostly flat.

Make a number of drawings, all in rectangles, using different views. Dispense with the viewfinder and rely increasingly on judging the arrangement with the eyes unaided. Gradually add a little more detail, and try to shade so that distant parts look as though they are distant. Use the medium which is most natural for you. Use line, or shading, thick or thin, heavy or light, according to your natural instincts and, by the same instincts, begin to decide on a favourite size for your drawings.

At this point it will be appreciated that the drawings, so far, have been done without considering them as designs for tapestries. On the whole, this is the best way to draw. An artist who draws is a predator, consuming what is seen, digesting it, and allowing it time to settle down and to be transformed, slowly, into ideas for painting, tapestry, ceramics, jewellery, sculpture or any other field in the visual arts.

The themes covered in the experiments have been Still Life, Plants and Trees, Flowers, Faces, Figures, Landscape. These range across most visual experiences, and within them you might feel to be drawn in a particular direction. The choice can be made clearer by writing a table of

	interested	which	where	interested in now
Faces	✓			
single figures	✓			
groups of figures				
Flowers				
what sort?				
Plants				
what kind?				
Trees				
groups of trees	✓			
groups of bushes				
Animals	✓	) cats		
which?		) sheep		
Birds				
Insects				
Landscape	✓		hills and lakes)	✓
what sort? where?			Cumbria)	
Seascape	✓			
where?				
Townscape				
where?				
Still life / objects				

choices, similar to that in figure 65, where the possibilities for one artist are classified, with a decision in the final column. This does not cut out the option to develop other interests at a later date. Jotting down ideas in words can be as useful as sketches on some occasions.

Experiment 15
Decide on a theme. At first, keep the drawing to a few basic shapes which represent the contents accurately. Give thought to the shapes in between, and to the shapes along the edges of

65 A table of interests

the rectangle. Balance the arrangement to your satisfaction before combining line and shading and working towards the smaller shapes and details. Spend a considerable time on this drawing, and continue to add detail until as much information as possible has been included. This process entails looking hard, and long, at everything. Small details should be drawn as confidently as the big shapes, treating them as big shapes in miniature.

Experiment 16

Choose part of the drawing done in Experiment 15. Enlarge this to fill the rectangle for a new drawing, altering shapes a little, where necessary, to improve the arrangement. Use a series of shaded and graded tones to make a balanced tonal arrangement. Use different sorts of contrasts, quite deliberately: dark against white, grey against grey, white against grey, dark against grey. Start another drawing, repeating the situation, but this time selecting, for enlargement, part of the drawing you have just completed. It is possible, therefore, that only two or three shapes will be involved. Balance and contrast carefully.

Experiment 17

Experiments 1 to 16 have been based on direct observation: observing and drawing a given situation. It is fruitful, sometimes, to observe first and to draw later. This can be called indirect observation. A period of observation is followed by a period of gestation, which is followed by drawings done, usually, in quite a different place from that in which the observations were made. Most of the illustrations in this book are based on this sort of indirect observation of Cumbrian landscape. Over a period of years, it became usual to notice new things and to register them mentally in terms of never having quite seen it like that before. On one visit the dark stone walls were seen as dark lines; on another visit the lighter lines of paths on the hills were most important. They were sometimes developed into drawings weeks or months later, when the initial observation sprang back into the memory. Drawing from indirect observation is not just drawing from memory, however. No attempt is made to recall everything seen. The aim is to concentrate, in the first place, on observing, letting the interest wander around, until something stands out from the rest, or until there is a feeling of grasping what is being looked at. There should be no great effort to catalogue everything. In some way it is like using film: the film keeps the record, depending on what the camera was pointing at. The image is

developed later, and is subject to variable light and exposure.

For this experiment, choose what is to be looked at in terms of your main visual interest, as discussed in Experiment 15, and then sit in front of it, or walk round it, or through it. Do this on several occasions, with intervals between, so that the theme gets into your system, becomes part of you. Then sit down with drawing paper in front of you, well away from what you have been looking at. Start to draw fairly lightly, in a rectangle, as before. Do not rub out. When you begin to identify a shape, which is growing on the paper, draw with rather more strength, in order to clarify it. It should perhaps be stressed, that this is not some sort of mystical experience, nor is it automatic drawing. Once a shape becomes recognisable, there will be visual memories to reinforce it. It is likely that the larger shapes will come together fairly early, but this is by no means a rule. What is important is that, however the shapes arrive, your concern for balancing shapes and tones, to make a satisfactory arrangement, should match your concern for using a personal theme.

Experiment 18

Make a drawing, from indirect observation, using shading only. One result of this experiment is illustrated in figure 66. The theme is landscape. The landscape walked through is in the region of Grasmere, in Cumbria. The drawing tools were 0.50 mm and 1.00 mm Rotring 2000 Isograph pens, which give a uniform black line, suitable usually for diagrams, but used here to facilitate clear black and white reproduction. The drawing was started in the top right hand corner, the pen being used by the left hand. As the drawing progressed, in blocks of tone, steps were taken back towards the top, and further areas of tone were added. The idea of cloud and hill tops came about one third of the way down, and the patch of dark, towards the lower right corner, suggested part of a lake. No attempt was made to clarify, with outlines, after the impression of the bulk of the hills, and the effect of light, had been achieved. The working time was about

54

66 *Opposite:* A line drawing of a landscape

67 Tapestry: 'Islands', 165 cm × 120 cm (5 ft 6 in × 4 ft)

four hours. There is an affinity between this kind of free, but structured drawing, and the tapestry in figure 67. Both start from the same ideas, and develop them. But each is developed in terms of its own medium and techniques. The drawing does not imitate tapestry weaving and the tapestry does not imitate drawing.

For the experiment, choose the drawing tools which you like most. Start at any point in the rectangle, and let the shading progress according to the medium. In the case of pastel, for example, shading can be rubbed in, or can be linear. Pencil can be rubbed with a wet rag or finger. Take risks and do not be afraid of spoiling the work at any stage.

Experiment 19
Explore a theme, using indirect observation. Try to confine the drawing to line, so that the result is more linear than shaded. Link many of the lines to the edges of the rectangle, and draw in complete shapes if possible.

Experiment 20
Continue indirect observation, and use both line and shading, aiming always for a well-balanced, structured arrangement. Experiments 1 to 19 are concerned with looking at the natural world, and selecting from it, by drawing it. Some competence will, by now, have been achieved, if the experiments have been carried out conscientiously. At this point, a wider acquaintance with the work of some other visual artists will be useful. A number of suggestions follow, which are meant to act as pointers to some of the directions which can be taken to assist further personal development. They are not meant to be read consecutively, but can be noted, or ticked, on reading through, and those which appeal can be taken up.

1 Keep a notebook/sketchbook, which is a dated record. It can include written comments, sketches, ideas to pursue, postcards, photographs; anything which contributes, in your opinion, to growing visual interest.

2 Visit all kinds of exhibitions: national and local art galleries, and smaller art galleries and art shops, anywhere where drawings and paintings are exhibited. Look at pictures in other people's houses. The real excitement of discovering work, which speaks to your own condition, is just as likely to come in a small art gallery as in a major exhibition. Sometimes there is a need to see a great deal of other people's work; at other times there may be periods when, in order to make progress with ideas which are self-sufficient, seeing other work may be a distraction. Working as an artist does not mean being a reviewer, a critic, a historian, or a teacher, all of whom have to be constantly familiar with much that is going on in their fields; it means being obsessed with a particular kind of imagery, following your own eyes, and your own quirks, living and working in your own mental and visual territory.

3 Deepen your understanding of representational art. From good reproductions of drawings copy three or more, in order to appreciate more fully how the artist selected and represented what he was seeing. Some suggested combinations: Ingres, Rembrandt, van Gogh; Renoir, Dürer, Leonardo da Vinci. Look for contrasting combinations. Compare a figure drawing by Giacometti, for example, with one by David Hockney. Through copying, for the sake of understanding, it will be easier to see what they represent.

4 Make a pencil study of a Cubist painting, e.g. 'Portrait of Ambrose Vollard', by Picasso. Make a further study of Cézanne's portrait of the same Vollard. See Plates 20 and 21 of *Cubism*, by Edward Fry (Thames and Hudson, World of Art Library).

5 The use of perspective in art was discovered in the fifteenth century. It is still used, and some knowledge of it is essential to a draughtsman. Make tracings of some paintings or drawings which will illustrate the points at which lines vanish and where the eye level of the onlooker can be estimated easily. For example, in figure 68, 'The flagellation of Christ' by Piero della Francesca, lines indicate the vanishing point, on the eye level.

6 Figure 69 uses observed elements and

shapes, which are more symbolic than real. This is emphasised by the circle which dominates the lower half of the tapestry. No lake or tarn is quite so round, although seen from above some are nearly circular. This one is perched like a circular mirror against a red, black and brown landscape, with a dark stone wall, several paths and a hill, clouds and sky. The circle contains an inner seascape, a grey reflection, which can be read as a non-figurative arrangement. A red, pink and grey sun drops through the left-hand side, but not as a sunset. It is seen partly through a lens, which produces two hexagonal shapes, an effect which occurs only in photographs and films. Essentially this is a simple decorative wall hanging, but it can be understood on more than one level. It is difficult to impose a structure which is partly symbolic and partly abstract on representational ideas or elements, unless there is a strong natural inclination in this direction on the part of the

68 Perspective diagram of 'The flagellation of Christ' by Piero della Francesca

designer-weaver. See works by Paul Gauguin, Odelon Redon, Paul Klee and Max Ernst (particularly his work from the 1950s).

7 In figure 70 the lower half of a circle represents a lake, with reflections and movements of water. In the middle section four white roads fade into a group of triangles, based on the gable ends of houses. The fairly severe treatment of the half circle changes to a softer area under the roads. There is an almost naturalistic version of hills above. There is some depth in the sea and sky, but the stripes are like a conventional rug. This illustrates how a variety of influences come together in a personal 'style'.

As an experiment modulate a rectangle into simple divisions: squares, stripes, circles, half-circles, horizontals. Draw into this a theme using

69 *Opposite*: Tapestry: 'Grey tarn', 90 cm × 150 cm (3 ft × 5 ft)

70 Tapestry: 'Roads into a village', 165 cm × 120 cm (5 ft 6 in × 4 ft)

some of your favourite ideas or objects, marrying it with the structure in some way.

As an alternative experiment, take a completed drawing and see what underlying structure can be emphasised, by drawing over it with bold lines, or on tracing paper which has been fixed over the drawing. Now repeat the original drawing, but keep the emphasis on the structure until there is a balance between structure and representation.

8 Abstract art does not invoke the real, or make reference to it. 'Black square on a white ground', was painted before 1920 by the Russian painter Malevitch. Between 1920 and 1940 the Dutch painter, Mondrain, restricted his forms to the purely geometrical. Another Russian painter, Kandinsky, did his first abstract in 1910. Look at work by these painters. All three relinquished representational painting in different ways. If abstract art appeals to you, it is, perhaps, best to be influenced by the early practitioners. Among English artists, Ben Nicholson, who painted attractive decorative landscapes and still lifes, came under the purist influence of Mondrain and moved into abstract paintings and reliefs.

Some experiments, which demonstrate basic ideas to follow, for those who wish to have immediate practical work:

(i) Divide a rectangle into two, then three, then five or so divisions, allowing always for a good asymmetrical balance of shapes.

(ii) Divide rectangles symmetrically, vertically and horizontally and then subdivide the resulting rectangles asymmetrically.
Shade to make a balance of form and tone.

(iii) Cut five abstract, irregular shapes, from pieces of brown paper, and arrange them in a rectangle. Try out various arrangements, before sticking them down.

(iv) Cut or tear five abstract, irregular shapes, from white paper. Shade four of them in a graded tonal scale. Shade a rectangle in a darker tone, and arrange the shapes inside it, including the white one, and stick them down.

(v) Draw a number of loosely-made abstract shapes inside a rectangle, to make an arrangement of small forms in a big space. The shapes need not look flat, but can be shaded to give variety and depth.

(vi) Draw a number of loosely-made abstract shapes inside a rectangle, to make an arrangement of small and large shapes.

(vii) Using compasses, or drawing free hand, arrange a number of interlocking, overlapping circles, inside a rectangle. Make further concentric circles within them. Divide some, with spokes from the centre. Shade some of the shapes.

(viii) Search through a well-illustrated history of art, and make notes on abstract forms of art, going back to antiquity. Note particularly the art of Islam.

(ix) Architecture is abstract in its essentials. Make studies of buildings, or parts of buildings, plotting accurately the proportions of shapes in relation to each other.

(x) Sculpture, painting, pottery and textiles, in early cultures, or in primitive cultures, are often near to abstraction, while representing birds, animals, plants and the human figure. The forms and decorations express the native mythology. Make studies of those which appeal to you aesthetically. Take one of these studies and, although the mythological significance is lost, develop it into an abstract design.

9 In the daydreaming, soporific state, before falling fully asleep, or on waking, it is sometimes noticed that strange connections are made between pieces of visual experience. The same is true of remembered dreams. In 1924 Surrealism emerged as a movement, with a Manifesto, in which dream and reality were embraced as a new sort of reality. Some of the works of Max Ernst, Marc Chagall, Giorgio da Chirico, Paul Delvaux, Yves Tanguy, Rene Magritte, Salvador Dali, Marcel Duchamp and Joan Miro form a rich mine for those who are able to take a leap, imaginatively, out of a rational, ordered world.

Try to make a series of drawings in which you let ideas come together, without making conscious decisions, getting as near to a daydreaming state as possible. If this is not possible, choose a few small objects at random. Draw them, without thinking too much about planning the arrangement, and introduce any other ideas which come by association as you are working.

10 Observe things in motion. Television can be helpful here. The idea is to see lines of movement, particularly swift or violent movement. Some photographers have made records, in the form of multiple exposures, of figures in motion, and painters have become involved in the idea of speed. A short-lived Italian movement, Futurism, started in 1909, and aimed to express the spirit of modern life, its fever and speed. Boccioni's sculptures and paintings are the most typical. Multiple images are part of every-day experience. If a hand is held up about 30 cm (1 ft) from the face, and the eyes are focused on an object at the other side of the room, it is possible to observe, in a detached sort of way, that there is also visible a double image of the hand. If the focus is switched to the hand, the object in the distance is seen double. If the hand is moved from side to side, while focusing on it, it has several images, and the distant object remains as a double image. Getting around would be confusing if this concentration on how we see were the norm. See 'Nude descending a staircase', by Marcel Duchamp, as an example of a painting using movement as its source.

In a series of drawings, experiment with ideas on motion, or on multiple images, applying them to your favourite thematic material. In the case of landscape, consider how the images change, as the head is moved, or as the body moves through the landscape. Perspective was referred to as having been invented. It implies a strict view through one eye in a fixed position, and contrasts strongly with the ideas under consideration now. It is, nonetheless, valid, as a secure way of ordering what we see.

Robert Delaunay, a French painter, said, 'colour alone is form and subject'. By 1912 he was making paintings of geometric abstracts which were patterns of colour. So far, in this section,

nothing has been said about colour. For the tapestry weaver there are enough natural fibres to make almost purely tonal weaving a full-time occupation. But the possibilities of dyeing, or buying coloured yarns, are unlimited. In Chapter 1 the section on dyeing suggested ways of exploring colour through the use of chemical dyes. If, however, drawing becomes a serious part of tapestry weaving, it is likely that some familarity with the basics of painting will be useful. The section which follows is, like the section on drawing, a starters' section, designed to given some confidence in beginning to use the tools and equipment of the painter.

Painting

It is recommended that a choice between water colour and gouache should be made. Oil painting is not really recommended for tapestry weavers. It is a matter of personal preference, of course, but it would seem that oil painting is the painter's medium, which requires time and attention that excludes time for tapestry weaving. There will be exceptions to this rule: probably experienced painters, who become interested in tapestry after considerable experience of painting.

Water colour
This is a translucent medium and should be used on white paper. It can be applied in single washes, or built up in several layers. It is best used, at first, with full, wet brushes, on a dry surface, but it can be used on a wet surface, when the colours mix by running into each other. The extent to which they run is dependent on the degree of wetness of both paper and brush. Wet on dry, and wet on wet, can be alternated in the same painting. Washes can be controlled by keeping a reservoir of colour at the lower edge of the wash, taking the wash from one side to the other and from top to bottom (see figure 71). Water colour is a medium which can be used for quick impressions, or for extended paintings, in considerable detail. As in the drawing experiments, be bold, rather

than cautious. As water colour dries to a lighter tone, keep this in mind when mixing the colours. Keep water colour brushes clean. If you want to be sure that the colour is pure and remains freshly translucent, only use the brushes for water colour. Do not use them for gouache, as traces of white will persist and cloud the water colour later. Paper should normally be stretched, both sides being soaked in clean water, after which it expands fully, lying flat on the board. Strips of gummed paper, pressed firmly all round, to grip both paper and board, will hold the paper as it dries. Sometimes, if the drying is too quick, or if the gummed paper is too thin, the paper will pull away as it dries, in which case the process has to be repeated, with a shorter period of soaking, or better gummed paper.

Gouache

This is water colour used with white, to make some parts opaque. Under various names it is sold as poster colour, or gouache colour, and in some forms it is waterproof, when dry, and known as acrylic gouache. Acrylic paints can be used, like gouache, on paper, but they are also used on canvas or board, and can be mixed with a special medium and used more after the manner of oil paints. So, for use in painting as a preliminary to tapestry weaving, ordinary gouache paints are preferable. Artists' quality paints are made with better, more reliably permanent, pigments. Gouache can be used in thin washes, like water colour, by adding water. But light tones can also be made by adding white. The colour should be kept workable, in a cream-like consistency, like table cream. It is possible to paint mixtures of light colours over dark ones, or directly on dark paper. When used in a creamy consistency, many gouache colours have enough density to cover darker areas. Brushes should be washed thoroughly in water after use, as the pigment tends to gather in the hairs, near the ferrule, and this rots the hairs. Paper can be stretched, but this is only necessary when the colour is being thinned a great deal with water, or when the paper is very thin.

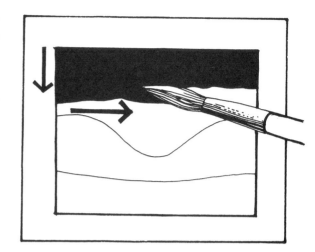

71 Putting on a water colour wash

In using either water colour or gouache, rely on a natural instinct for colour, if you feel that you have one. A number of experiments follow, which are based on a useful colour theory which can be referred to when natural instincts are jaded, or can be used as a foundation from which further personal work may grow.

Experiment 21

Figure 72 is a colour circle, divided into three primary and three secondary colours. Red, yellow and blue, when mixed in adjacent pairs, make orange, green and violet. Make a colour circle for reference. Adjust the primaries you are using until satisfactory secondaries have been mixed.

Experiment 22

Colours which are opposite to each other, in the circle, are complementary; that is, they give maximum contrast to each other. In a red tapestry, for example, a green shape will increase the redness of the red. In another, blue and green triangles at the top will have the effect of stimulating an area of pink immediately below. Pink belongs to the reds, and green is the complementary colour.

Mix light tones of one colour, and light tones of its complementary, and set them against each other by filling 5 cm (2 in) squares, cutting them

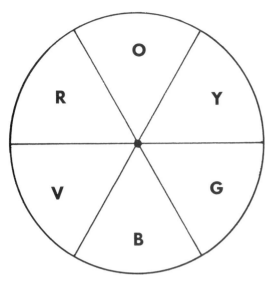

72 A colour circle

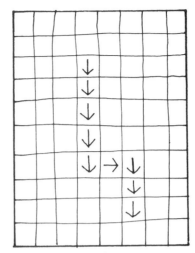

73 Diagram of a grid painting

out, moving them around and finally sticking them down.

Experiment 23
Divide a rectangle into squares by freehand drawing, each square being about 3 cm ($1\frac{1}{4}$ in). Start painting individual squares at any point, choosing a primary colour for the first square, then filling in a series of squares along a path of adjacent squares. See figure 73, in which the arrows indicate the progress of one path. Each succeeding square is a tone darker than the previous one, but the same primary colour is used throughout the path. Choose another primary for a second path, which can grow lighter or darker as it progresses. This should continue until all the squares have been filled. A freehand grid gives the painting an organic character. If this is not to your taste, divide the rectangle into squares with a ruler, and measure the 3 cm ($1\frac{1}{4}$ in) squares exactly. A variation is to start the paths with light tones. For example, if using water colour start with a pale wash and add more colour as you move along the path. When full saturation of the colour has been reached add a little black, or some of the complementary colour, to make darker tones. If using gouache add a little of the chosen colour to white at the start, and then increasing amounts of the colour. After reach-

ing full saturation add a little black, and so on, until the colour is about to vanish into blackness. Black can be criticised because it tends to make water colour dirty and dead. Try a little of the complementary colour too, and use the black with care.

A further variation is to extend the range of colours by adding different yellows, reds, blues and greens, which have different pigment bases. The colours which are asterisked, in the following list, make a basic palette, but it is a good principle to look through the stock in your art shop and buy any colour which is attractive to you:

Yellows:	Lemon*, Cadmium*, Chrome, Aureolin, Ochre, Raw Sienna*, Raw Umber;
Reds:	Scarlet Lake*, Vermilion, Cadmium, Alizarin, Permanent Rose*;
Blues:	Cobalt, Ultramarine*, Prussian*, Antwerp, Manganese;
Greens:	Viridian*, Olive, Sap, Hookers dark* and light;
Browns:	Light Red, Burnt Sienna, Burnt Umber*, Sepia, Vandyke Brown, Venetian Red;
Greys:	Payne's Grey;
Blacks:	Lamp, Ivory*.

Some interesting variations in the use of the grid can be found in the paintings of the German artist, Paul Klee.

Experiment 24

Take Experiment 18, and repeat it by painting, instead of shading, laying down areas, or washes, of colour. It will be easier if the colours are limited in number but, as the object is to gain some control over the medium and to experience colour, your personal choice of bright or muted colour is important. Try out various ways of blending the colours: wet against wet, wet in dry, dragging a dryish brush across a dry wash, stippling, blotting.

Experiment 25

The experiments so far in this section use colour which is to be found in the paint box, rather than in external objects or in natural surroundings. The use of colour can be the result of direct or indirect observation, using those terms as they were used in the section on drawing.

(i) Take a leaf or a flower. Observe the colours, and try to match them, one by one. Paint in blobs of colour, putting the blobs side by side, as a catalogue of the colours in the object.

(ii) After the previous experiment, draw the leaf or flower, but this time paint in the colours where they occur, as you observe them. The original drawing can be done with a brush, in a pale colour, using the point of the brush to make an expressive line.

(iii) Draw a loaf of bread, and paint it, observing carefully the colour and tone changes. Do not be over-anxious to make it accord to some idea of 'real' which probably equates with a colour photograph. This may be how it will appear finally, but if your concern is with matching colour and tone, you can leave the 'real' aspects of it to take care of themselves. The finished painting will not look like a loaf of bread, but like a painting of a loaf of bread.

Other themes, more to your own personal liking, can now be taken, in a continuation of these experiments in painting. Avoid too much detail in any preliminary drawing; allow the colour to supply the detail. It can also be interesting, and may suit your way of working, to dispense with preliminary drawing, building up an impression of things in patches of colour, adding and over-painting, here and there, where it seems appropriate.

Experiment 26

As in Experiment 17, spend some time getting familiar with a theme. This time, however, concentrate on impressions and sensations of colours. Later, in a neutral setting for preference, begin to paint. There are many ways to go about this. It may, however, be best to use the number 10 brush or the one-stroke brush for painting in some large areas with washes of colour, which are mixed as a result of the earlier observations. At some point a structure will become apparent, as an attempt is made to define the shapes which filter through the memory.

Several small scale paintings (about 20 cm × 15 cm, 8 in × 6 in), could be made, unless you want to paint on a larger format on bigger sheets of paper. It is worth repeating that you should work, at all times, on a size which you can cope with. If you feel that you are being too cautious, try something bigger. If you feel comfortable and in control, do not be persuaded to change. There are no rules about this. Nor are there rules about colour. The experience of complementary colours and the colour circle might be a guide and a help in solving problems; but the choice—muted colours, bright, or loud, strident colours, gentle harmonies, daring contrasts—should be very personal.

The work in tapestry weaving proceeds alongside the activities in drawing and painting, and it is likely that the choice of colours in wool will be influenced by your paintings, while your paintings are likely to be influenced by the sorts of colours you use in weaving. In both activities, in consequence, the colours are likely to be all the more interesting.

3 DESIGNING AND WEAVING TAPESTRIES

Designing

The celebrated Egyptian children of the Harrania Tapestry Workshops weave without preliminary drawings. Ramases Wissa Wassef, who started them in tapestry weaving in the 1940s and supports their work, feels that this makes their tapestries more spontaneous. There are, he says, difficulties which tend to destroy spontaneity whenever one draws up a plan. He reminds us that mediaeval tapestries were sometimes the result of simple verbal instructions, or a rough draft. Working from the material itself, and taking risks, stimulates and disciplines creative effort. His views, in his particular situation, are vindicated by the results in the tapestries woven by the children.

Not everyone can weave spontaneously but, occasionally, it is a good idea to try it. There is a degree of involvement and commitment, which can be exhilarating, in starting a tapestry, however small or however big, at the bottom and working to the top, weaving without preliminary drawing or designing. It is an excellent way to learn about the possibilities and limitations of tapestry techniques. It illustrates, practically and very clearly, that tapestry weaving and drawing/painting are each activities in their own right, exploring common ground in different ways. Sometimes, however, it is necessary to plan a tapestry and to make a full scale drawing, or cartoon, to guide the weaving. A cartoon can be a simple statement of a basic layout, within the limits of which much spontaneous weaving can take place, or it can be detailed. For the individual tapestry weaver, who is also the designer, it is vital to choose a method which is not restricting or inhibiting and which does not lead to mechanical copying of a design, however good it might be.

It is assumed at this stage in your work, facing a new warp on the loom, that you have settled on a theme, and that you have some familiarity with the various techniques through practical experiments on a sampler or a piece of free weaving. You will also have several drawings or paintings around the theme, which you are ready to view as ideas for a tapestry.

The immediate objective should be to make a layout, or basic structure, which will leave out all details which you sense are too complicated to weave easily. In addition, all steep angles and most verticals should be modified or left out. It might seem that this takes the essentials out of your drawing or painting, and that you are left with an elementary version which you could easily have put together without wasting time observing and becoming deeply involved with the theme. It would be a mistake to reach this conclusion. This is a difficult and important stage in the whole process of drawing, painting, designing and weaving. Without the prelimi-

nary involvement in the theme and the gathering of information, and the imaginative experiments preceeding the tapestry, the simple layout would be an empty and contrived arrangement of a few shapes. The simplification which is now being concentrated on is to be the result of knowledge and experience of both ideas and techniques. So, with this in mind, it is best to be ruthless in simplifying and altering, if necessary, so that the transition or bridge between the drawing/painting and tapestry is a 'pregnant' statement and a starting point for the new medium.

Figure 74 is a drawing in pencil, pastel and

74 *Opposite:* A drawing for a tapestry

75 A drawing in Cumbria

wax. Figures 75, 76, 77, 78 and 79 are examples of a preoccupation with similar elements in landscape: paths, hills, lake, trees, reflections. From these earlier drawings grew the idea for a number of tapestries, which were done over several years. Figure 74 is a drawing which is half-way to the tapestry, but no attempt has been made to disguise it. Figure 80 is the simplified drawing, which was enlarged to full scale and fixed behind the warp. Figure 81 is a photograph of the tapestry which is nearest to the cartoon, hanging in a domestic setting, but figures 82 and 83 are derived from the same source. These tapestries will be referred to later. For the moment it is, perhaps, clear that figure 74 is a transitional drawing, and that figure 80 is the starting point for the weaving process.

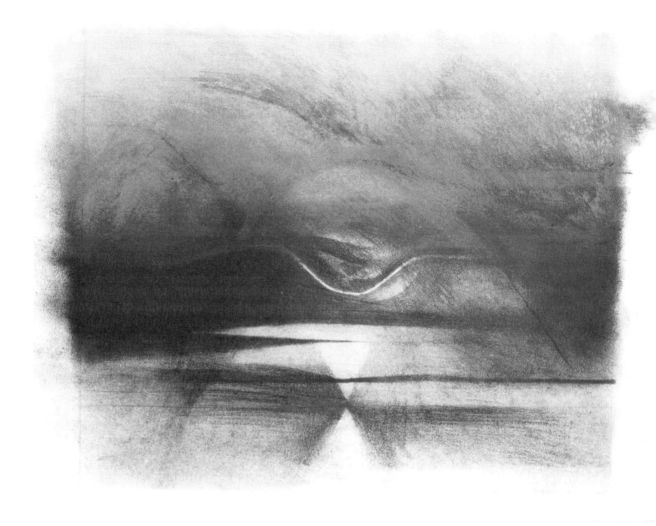

76 Drawing: 'By a lake'

77 Drawing: 'Road by a lake'

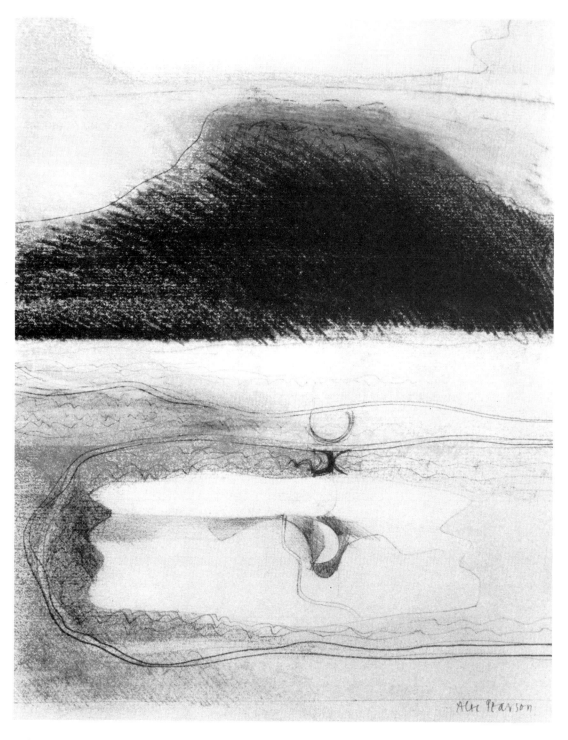

78 Drawing: 'Hill and small tarn'

79 *Opposite: Drawing: 'Hill and lake'*

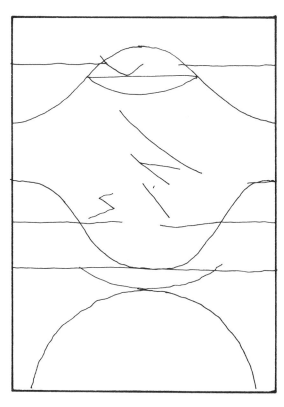

80 Simple version of figure 74

81 *Opposite:* A tapestry *in situ*

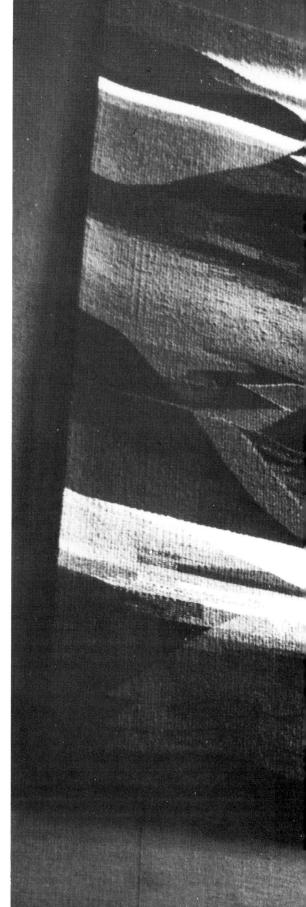

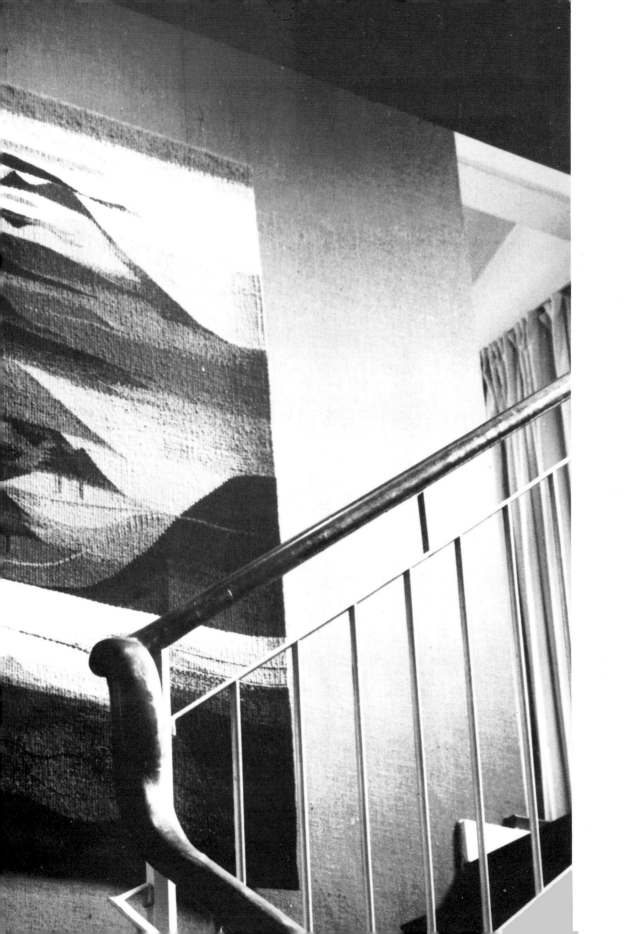

74

83 Tapestry: 'Cumbrian landscape', 150 cm × 180 cm
(5 ft × 6 ft)

82 Tapestry: 'Wood in Cumbria', 165 cm × 120 cm
(5 ft 6 in × 4 ft)

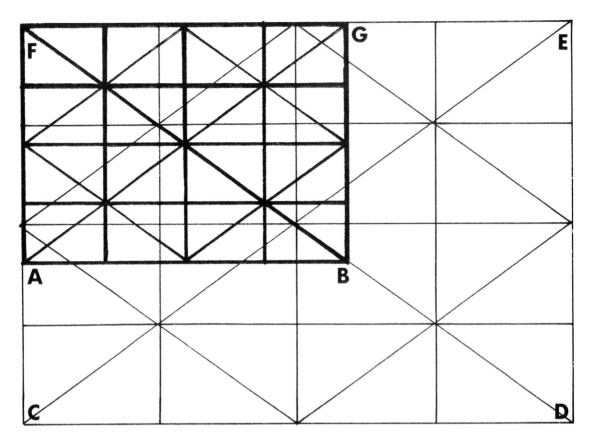

In order to enlarge a drawing to a full-size cartoon, for fixing behind the warp, draw a rectangle the size of the proposed tapestry on a sheet of paper, using a felt pen. A pencil line can be used first and blacked in afterwards. If the tapestry is to be bigger than the sheet of paper stick several sheets together, edge to edge, using adhesive tape on the back of the sheets. Draw a diagonal from corner to corner. Refer to figure 84, where the diagonal is FD, within the rectangle FCDE. Draw the second diagonal CE. Through the centre of the rectangle make a horizontal and vertical line from side to side and top to bottom. Draw the diagonals in the resulting four quarters, and divide again with horizontal and vertical divisions. The small rectangle in figure 84, FABG, is the drawing which is being enlarged. This is subdivided in exactly the same way as the large rectangle. This system can be used for all enlarging and reducing. FABG is a drawing. To enlarge it

84 Enlarging a drawing

85 *Opposite:* A drawing ready for enlarging

proportionally to any size, project FA to the required length FC. Project the diagonal FB. Draw a line at right angles to FC and project it to meet the diagonal at D. Then connect ED.

Suppose that FCDE is a very large drawing which is to be reduced proportionally. Draw the diagonal FD. Shorten the line FC to the required length FA. Draw AB at right angles to FA. Connect GB at right angles to FE.

In the rectangle FABG, on a separate sheet (see figure 85), make the simple line drawing of the proposed tapestry. Draw the lines in firmly, being quite decisive about the shapes and the way they relate to the edges of the rectangle. Draw the diagonals and subdivide FABG until it has 32 triangles of the same size. Enlarge this drawing on the larger full size sheet and

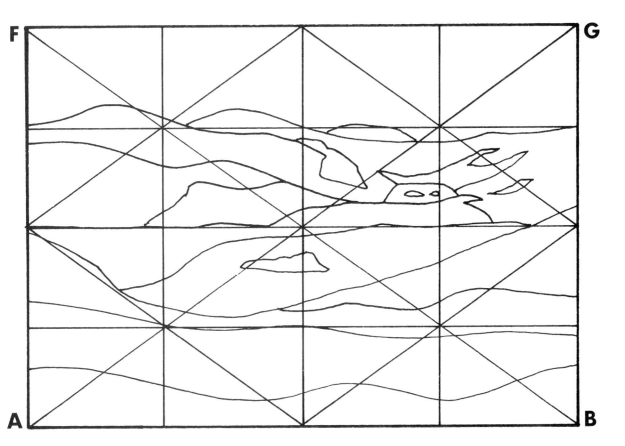

F   G

A   B

emphasise the design by marking on top of the pencil lines with a felt pen. Fix the sheet behind the warp on the loom. This can be done effectively by suspending a length of wood and pinning the sheet on it, using drawing pins or staples along the top edge. Adjust the sheet so that the rectangle coincides with the weaving area, ensuring that the sides are vertical and that the warp ends at each side (the selvedges) lie along the lines marking the edge of the design. Finally, mark the drawing on the actual warp threads, with a felt pen or brush. Key points should be marked all the way round the warp thread, because of the possible twisting of the warp ends during the weaving.

It is possible to make the enlargement directly onto the warp, using the enlarging method discussed above. A long straight stick is essential for ruling along the lines, particularly on large tapestries. After the grid and triangles have been marked out it is advisable to keep

the enlargement of the drawing to a few shapes initially, because of the difficulties of drawing small shapes across the warp threads. In making the original drawing, with this need for clear shapes in mind, the importance of thinking in terms of the scale or size of the tapestry cannot be emphasised too much. An original drawing, which works on its own scale, has to be interpreted and if necessary regrouped to work on the scale of the tapestry. Interpretation starts at this point. However skilfully the weaver interprets the details of the drawing, if the scale is wrong at the outset and adjustments are not made as soon as this fact begins to emerge, little can be done at a later stage to save the work. It will always look wrong at a distance. A preliminary drawing 33 cm × 18 cm (1 ft 1 in × 7 in) looks somewhat different when enlarged to 330 cm × 180 cm (11 ft × 6 ft). Some designers are able to plan directly on a sheet or a warp this size (say 330 cm × 180 cm) from the start of the work, but it is more likely for most people that the only possible way to arrive at the full size is by way of smaller drawings. Having reached full size, however, time must be spent viewing the work and making adjustments. These adjustments should not be thought of in terms of more or less detail, although there will be the temptation to do just this. It is vague, but correct, to talk about 'the feel of the thing' being right or not. 'It feels right like this' is the conclusion to be reached. And alterations must be made to that end.

Continuous redesigning during the weaving process can keep the options open. This has little to do with the question of scale referred to above. As the tapestry grows up the loom, the appearance of the weft face weave takes on its own character, which will influence thoughts about what follows in the next few inches. New thoughts occur and these should not be rejected, any more than they were rejected while drawing or painting. This is vital to the progress of the work. There is nothing preordained. Tapestry weaving is not cloth weaving, in which quantities have to be worked out and plans adhered to once they have been thoroughly thought through. The history of tapestry is rooted in the history of painting, and the individual designer-weaver is in a unique position of thinking through and making changes right to the end of the piece.

A stimulating variation is to draw only about 25 per cent of the idea on the warp at the start, developing the rest as the weaving goes up. It is easy in practice to select the right lines among several try-outs. The amount of detail in the drawing at this stage is dependent on the need for guiding lines. A constant interplay between weaving and drawing may be the method in one section of the tapestry. At other times, reference to the drawing may be minimal.

Weaving

The techniques illustrated in Chapter 1 are not usually all in use in every tapestry. In this section several tapestries will be described and

illustrated, but first a general description of the weaving of a typical piece will cover some of the situations which are common to the weaving of tapestries. At the end of Chapter 1 the loom was ready, the warp evenly taut. At the end of the last section either the cartoon was in position, with some drawing carried out on the warp threads, or it had been decided not to use a cartoon or a preliminary drawing. At all events, the idea, the warp and the wool for the weft were all ready.

Starting at one side the fingers open the shed and the handskein or ball, or bobbin, of wool is passed along. About 8 cm (3 in) should be left hanging at the front. Later this can be threaded up along the selvedge, inside the weft, and

86 Threading weft yarn end into the selvedge

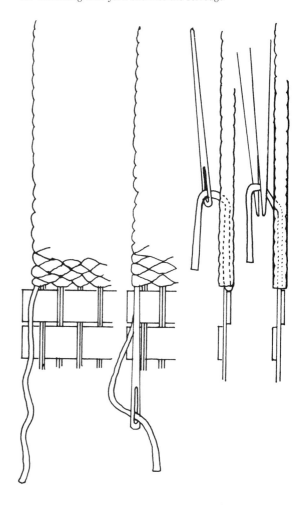

taken out at the back (see figure 86) to secure it. In the early stages try to keep the width exactly right. Measure it at 1 cm (or $\frac{1}{2}$ in) intervals. The weft should be looped along each pick (figure 87) and pressed down with the tips of the fingers. It should be neither tight nor slack but should pass between the warp ends comfortably (figure 88). If it is too tight it will pull the warp out of true and eventually pull in the selvedge and narrow the tapestry; if it is too slack the tapestry will get wider. It would be good to think that this is always perfectly under control. In practice the control of weft tension is a variable, particularly when many small shapes are being woven, but the aim should always be to get it right.

The first 2.5 cm to 5 cm (1 in to 2 in) of plain tapestry weave makes a suitable hem. One or two picks of darker wool can be woven next to indicate where the hem should be turned for stitching. Check that this line is at right angles to the selvedge. From time to time the general progress of the weaving should be checked in this way, to ensure that the picks are being built up at right angles to the selvedge, or parallel to the base line. Following the hem line a few more centimetres of plain tapestry weave will give the piece a firm foundation. If the curves and diagonals of a design spring from the base line it is sometimes difficult to keep it flat. A step at the bottom edge tends to bulge outwards. The plain weave holds the work together.

87 Controlling weft tension

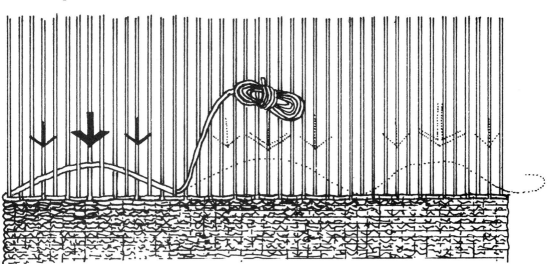

88 Weft in relation to warp ends seen from above or below

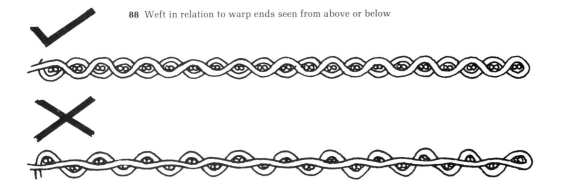

As shapes are introduced it is reasonable and safe to build them up above the level of the surrounding shapes. This is not approved of by all tapestry weavers, some of whom insist on building up the work as nearly horizontally as possible, so as to keep the weft tension evenly distributed. There is some good sense in this, of course. When a shape is built up above the general level there is a tendency for each succeeding step to pull the warp ends closer together within the woven shapes. This means that when the adjacent areas are woven the weft has to cope with wider gaps between warp ends and the resulting ridges are slightly curved. Nevertheless, it is always tempting to build up certain shapes and there is an advantage in doing so: the background colour can be chosen to complement an already woven shape more effectively than if all shapes progress equally. In spontaneous weaving this is especially the case. There is no need to be over anxious about weft tension. Practice develops a feeling for it. Being over anxious tends to make things worse, as the stress is communicated through the fingers. Figure 89 shows a large frame loom with a typical building up sequence on a 180 cm × 120 cm (6 ft × 4 ft) tapestry. Built-up shapes must always get progressively narrower, leaving the surrounding warp ends free, so that the shed can be opened easily by the fingers. Overhanging shapes (see figure 90) do not allow the filling in of adjacent areas without recourse to a laboriously slow needle weaving technique.

If the fingers open the shed, without pulling the warp threads unduly forward, the tension of the warp will remain evenly taut. Keep a watch, however, for the odd thread which slackens, and tighten it. A narrow rod, or knitting needle, can be easily twisted in the offending warp end and anchored, as in figure 91, under other warp ends at the bottom of the loom. If a group of ends slackens, lengths of card, or very thin strips of wood, may be pushed up under the warp until they sit on the top bar. Failure to keep an eye on the tension of the warp as a whole can result in bulging areas in the finished work. I always found it reassuring, in my early

89 *Opposite*: Building up a shape on the loom

90 Overhanging or undercutting shapes

91 A way of tightening a warp end

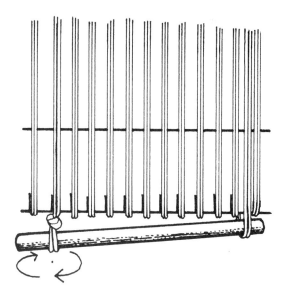

experiences as a tapestry weaver, that more experienced weavers obviously do not always overcome these problems. The evidence is in the work. It should also be said that the final work is often none the worse, visually and aesthetically, for its technical lapses. And perhaps it should be agreed that apparently uneven weaving and undulating bottom edges can be the result of deliberate policy. Even so, the aim should be to be able to weave a straight edge, and a flat rectangular tapestry.

Around the half-way-up mark special attention must be paid to measuring the width. It is easy to forget this. The weaving sometimes goes, apparently, well and the ideas flow into an easy rhythm. And then suddenly, after ten centimetres, two have been lost or gained in the width. It is disappointing to have to pull back ten centimetres and it is a slow activity, which can result in the warp being pulled out of place, unless the weft is withdrawn very carefully.

When a mistake has been made (perhaps an area of colour turns out to be wrong), the weft can be pulled out easily, if it is cut every 15 cm (6 in) or so, with sharp scissors. The scissors cut across the weft vertically between the warp ends. At four ends per 2.5 cm (1 in) this is possible and has been done frequently without cutting the warp. But this is not particularly recommended. It requires undivided concentration, a steady hand and eye and perhaps also great impatience to get rid of the offending area, which overrides normal, cautious, good sense.

When changing colour leave about 8 cm (3 in) hanging down the back of the work. There is no need to wrap these ends round the warp, as subsequent picks pack the colour change point down firmly enough. Only when the tapestry is to be seen from both sides need they be threaded down inside the weft along the warp thread. It is sometimes recommended that the weft ends should hang down the weaver's side of the work, because the weft face is better on the back. But as this involves weaving the design back to front it can be a disadvantage. The cartoon would also have to be reversed. It makes for unnecessary complications, and it is more satisfactory to see the design growing as it

will hang and not marred by untidy bits of hanging wool which make it impossible to see adequately the parts which have been woven. This is also true of a design which is being woven sideways, to be hung eventually with the warp horizontal. It is best to be able to see the progressive stages of the work, to be able to judge it as a painter judges work in progress, unencumbered by a technical and historical dictate. Hackles might be raised about this. It is possible to weave in reverse on a horizontal or vertical loom, and to watch the weft face on the back of the loom in a mirror. This is the traditional method. It is a matter of choice today. If the finished work looks satisfactory, and hangs satisfactorily, it does not matter if the weaver did it in reverse in a mirror, doing a head stand, looking sideways, or on two feet looking at the front of the loom. It is interesting to try out all methods and to compare the results. I have found it impossible to work with the design in reverse and the weft ends hanging in front; and it is uncomfortable to weave the design sideways on. As explained, it was necessary to do this in the past, when very wide tapestries were made to fill walls, and when the width of the loom could often accommodate the height of the tapestry. Most of us are unlikely to be faced with such widths and, even if we are, it is quite natural to design in sections, which can be stitched together later.

When weaving a big area in one colour break the weft from time to time. This allows a certain easing of the tension, which can become tighter during the weaving of the area. It is also good to pause from time to time. Breaking the yarn encourages this. If it is realised that about 900 square cm (1 square ft) per working day is the average speed of weaving, using the techniques in this book, it can be readily seen that the weaving has to proceed evenly, but not for several hours without a break. About every hour a ten minute break should be taken, time enough for the arm and shoulder muscles to relax and the eyes to change focus. This advice is, of course, more for the full-time weaver than for someone who does a little in the evening and at week-ends. But muscles, eyes and tautness

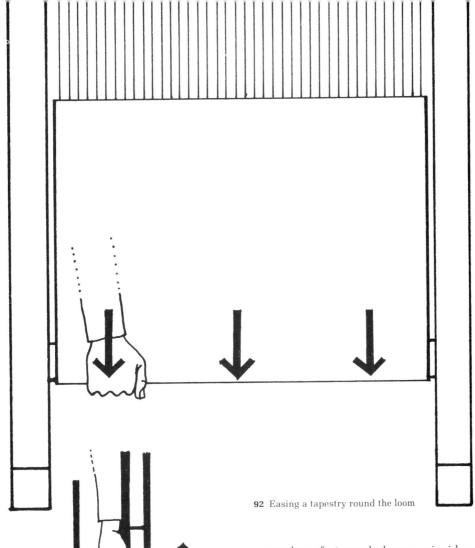

92 Easing a tapestry round the loom

a number of stepped shapes coincide or when the warp is fine and closely spaced. This has already been referred to but, as it is so important, it should be stressed again, at this point, that the weft should not be beaten down too firmly (as in rug weaving). But the warp must be covered. In the past tapestry weavers called inadequately covered warp 'lice'. We are not familiar with this visual experience these days. I was, however, impressed by this description when I saw lice on the long hairs of a black cat's back and was immediately reminded of a section of one of my early tapestries, in which a weft of black wool was too loosely packed down. The warp showed through in a mass of tiny lice-like points. As the tapestry grows, examine finished sections in a

apart, it is a good idea to break and to stand back and contemplate the work. Indeed, there are periods when the really hard work is being done when the weaver is contemplating the tapestry in its present state, rather than weaving relentlessly on. Weaving a large area in small sections is another way of getting an even overall weft tension. Although the fingers are normally adequate as tools for pressing down the weft, a pointed stick or the end of a bobbin can be used for small areas, particularly where

good light and press down offending picks. If you have overlooked an earlier section, the picks have to be realigned from that point up to the current weaving level. This can be a laborious and difficult operation. Evenness and consistency throughout should be aimed for from the start. As an experiment, on a small section of a warp or on a small frame, three areas can be woven: one too loosely packed, one too tightly and the final one half-way between.

Sometimes in a large tapestry double thickness wool may be in use. This obviously speeds up the weaving and enhances the texture from a tactile as well as a visual point of view. The extra thickness, however, may well be responsible for the 'lice' effect, especially if the weft tension is too tight. Extra long loops are advisable when laying in the picks and extra care in packing down.

Reference should be made to pulling the tapestry round the loom. If the finished tapestry is to be larger than two-thirds the height of the loom the warp will have to be slackened and the knots at the start and finish of the continuous warp untied. The work can then be eased down and round until a suitable weaving level has been reached. Levels and right angles should be checked carefully. At frequent intervals lay a straight stick or rule across the tapestry to ensure that the picks are straight and horizontal. See figure 92, where the arrows indicate two points at which a hand grasping the bottom edge of the work on the loom can ease the warp round. After retying the start and finish, test for correct tension throughout during the next 2.5 cm (1 in) of the weaving.

Towards the top of the tapestry there is a natural tendency to hurry, in order to see how the finished piece looks. Avoid this, otherwise the weft will become tighter and the width will narrow in the last few inches. Keep measuring the width or, if working with a cartoon, see that it is still in place, and be meticulous in observing the edges. If there is any doubt about tension it is best to keep it slightly slacker at the top. Allow a border for the top hem and make sure that this is planned carefully for the way you intend to hang the work.

93 Photograph: 'Lakes Grasmere and Rydal Water'

In order to explain some of the uses and developments of the techniques listed in Chapter 1, a number of tapestries are illustrated in the following pages, together with notes on their origin and reference to the designing and

weaving. This is necessarily a personal section. It is included in this manner, because a specific understanding of one designer-weaver's ways can sometimes stimulate another individual, not to copy but to have confidence in finding other ways. Often there are common starting points and approaches. When working in isolation, as many weavers do, there is a need to be reminded of this.

Figures 93, 94, 95 and 96. Photographs of Grasmere Lake, Rydal Water and tarns in nearby hills

94 Photograph: 'Small tarn on the fells'

95 Photograph: 'Tarn near Langdale-1'

96 Photograph:
'Tarn near Langdale-2'

97 Water colour: 'Reflection of a grid'

*Figures 97 and 98. Water colours based on
landscape near Grasmere*

98 Water colour: 'Moorland landscape'

99 Drawing: 'Village by a lake'

Figure 99. A drawing using the same source
The paintings and drawing were not based on these photographs but on the landscape which the photographs illustrate. The ruggedness, jagged shapes, undulating shapes, linear dark stone walls and lighter paths and the varying light are all characteristics of this part of the country. If the photographs are examined it will be seen that the smaller shapes are often miniatures of the larger shapes. There is a smoothness of undulation, combined with jagged minor shapes. The following tapestries are made of the same kinds of shapes, both small and large. Fundamentally, therefore, the photographs, paintings, the drawing and the tapestries are like each other. They are placed together at this point so that it is possible to see this by comparing details.

Figure 100. 'Tarns and hills'

This is a landscape within a landscape, the central parts being almost complete in themselves, as a landscape with its own sun and clouds, set in the larger framework of the hill. At the top of the hill is a tarn with an island in it (the long eye-like shape). In the lower half is a saucer shape, repeated. The lower saucer is a section of a tarn, which introduces a different dimension into the tapestry. On the whole, it is a decorative flat composition. Note, however, that the central area has small shapes in the tree, field and hill theme and that a certain depth is achieved where texture is used. Broken lengths of wool in dark and light are combined with one pick of light and one pick of dark, and then two picks of each (see Chapter 1, figures 13, 14 and 31). The shapes are all made of straight lines and curves, in which the steps range from one return round the warp end to about eight returns in the steepest part. This was largely a spontaneously woven piece, with some drawing done directly on the warp, but only as the work progressed. There was no preliminary cartoon. The height was not predetermined, but arrived at, when the arrangement seemed to be balanced and complete.

Figure 101. 'Tarns'

The saucer-like sections are repeated again here, the lower half of the tapestry representing a tarn, above which are the lines of paths set against hills. The tarn and island are also used again; above, in the top part, is an additional landscape with its own sun and moon, or moons, across which runs a final path. Apart from the lowest section there is very little texture: parallel lines (see figure 14) changing to small squares (figure 13). The techniques illustrated in figures 15, 16 and 17 are in evidence in the area below the main linear paths. The paths are built up as in figure 29.

Figure 102. 'Three islands'

This tapestry is dominated by a steep line. The steps are left as a series of slits. One side is darkness, the other daylight. Reference to the photograph of Grasmere and Rydal Water (figure 93) will indicate the origin: a lake with varied edges and a number of islands. In several areas the wool is used double thickness. This should show particularly clearly in the dome shape at centre right, which is woven with black and white wool twisted together. The textures (especially figure 13) are more in evidence in this piece. The black lines delineating the two dome-like hills at centre left make use of the laying-in technique of figures 29 and 33. There is a colour change in a chequered area above the dome-like hills. Yellow and green make this rather ambiguous as a shape. It could be fields, but the shape is like a flag blowing from a mast which is outside the frame of the tapestry on the left. The top section in particular attempts to cope with the rapidly changing moods of the landscape. This is a spontaneously woven piece. The one clear idea at the start was to make a steeply stepped division at some point.

Figure 103. 'Mountains with lake'

Woven soon after Figure 102, this tapestry makes use of the steep steps. There is hardly any texture outside the lake area at the bottom, which was woven from a hank which had been deliberately unevenly dyed. One half of the hank was given a longer period in the dye bath. This is a fairly haphazard way of building up a shape and a few inches need to be woven before a decision is made to carry on. The dark line, centre right, which crosses over several other shapes, has to be constructed with care. All the shapes under the line were woven first; the line was then laid in as a continuous weft of four picks, and the shapes above were filled in. The four stylised trees in the centre explain the contained landscape and allow the surrounding shapes to be read as hills and the horizontal stripes to be seen as water.

Figure 104. 'Roads by a lake'

This tapestry has much in common with figure 103: the contained landscape with trees, the use of undulating lines representing water, or walls, or paths and, in the case of the white lines which are angled as well as undulating, roads.

94

100 *Opposite:* Tapestry: 'Tarns and hills', 150 cm × 105 cm (5 ft × 3 ft 6 in)

101 Tapestry: 'Tarns', 150 cm × 90 cm (5 ft × 3 ft)

102 Tapestry: 'Three islands', 165 cm × 120 cm
(5 ft 5 in × 4 ft)

103 Tapestry: 'Mountains with lake', 165 cm × 120 cm
(5 ft 5 in × 4 ft)

105 Tapestry: 'Dwelling-place in hills', 139 cm × 172 cm
(4 ft 7 in × 5 ft 8 in)

104 *Opposite*: Tapestry: 'Roads by a lake',
165 cm × 120 cm (5 ft 5 in × 4 ft)

The most colourful area is the 'contained landscape', which has more detail than the rest of the work and is, in some sense, surrounded and enveloped by the other shapes. While the weaving was progressing the horizontal white line which fades into the right side of the hill was thought of as the surface of a lake, with the light reflected and sharply contrasting with the patch above the hills near the trees. The road dips suddenly to make a dramatic gesture against the dark of the main hill. The meaning which is attached to shapes by the weaver is not always conveyed to those who see the finished tapestry. This is not always important, but sometimes a title can give clues and many people are helped by some explanation.

Figure 105. 'Dwelling-place in hills'

Figure 106. 'Nomads' village'
Based on triangular shapes in the central areas, these two tapestries restrict textures to certain parts. In figure 105 the hill and cloud, and a small portion below the white undulating line to the left of where it thickens, make use of broken lengths of wool and of one pick of dark and one pick of light wool. And in the lower half of figure 106 there is a quantity of mixed black and white wool, and above the black line dividing off the lower third there is a repetition of visual texture from an unevenly dyed hank of wool. The rest is plain tapestry weave. The top section of figure 106 ends in a series of separate sections, which have long vertical slits dividing them. These represent a number of different, very simple landscapes, rather like a set of postcards propped up as an afterthought. The slits are a useful means of emphasising this. It was convenient to weave each landscape as a miniature tapestry.

Figure 107. 'Tarn on a hill'

Figure 108. 'Black fells'
The drawing (figure 107) is one of a series done in Cumbria, as a result of indirect observation while on a working visit. Grasses, or reeds growing in the water, were interpreted later in the tapestry, weaving initially a number of undulating lines (lower part of tarn towards the bottom of the tapestry) and above to the right, using the pick of dark followed by the pick of light, in undulations, to hint at verticality. There was something of an obsession with undulations and undulating lines. Had this obsession been conveyed through drawings which imitated tapestry weave there would have been an inhibiting influence at work. But as the weaving was spontaneous the natural direction and character of the weave could take over. A glance at the drawing in figure 107 will demonstrate that there are verticals in the work which were the natural thing to do in a drawing, but which would have been laborious and forced in a tapestry. There is also a softness in parts of the drawing, which could only have been imitated by the 'spotted dog' texture, which does service neither to drawing nor weaving.

Figure 109. 'Sea and islands'
Having referred to 'spotted dog' textures above it is appropriate to reproduce a tapestry in which texture was requested as part of the briefing for a commission. The colours range from white to creamy natural wools, greys, blacks and dyed blacks and browns. Short lengths of wool in varying tones were used for some textures, and the pick of dark and pick of light alternating to produce slightly chequered effects. But it was decided that a strong underlying structure should hold the textures together and that there should be areas of plain tapestry weave wherever possible. Figure 110, which is a detail of this tapestry, seen from an angle (which is how we see tapestries often enough) shows more clearly that every effort was made to control the texture within definite shapes. This is emphasised because it illustrates a point of view regarding texture. Some other weaver, including the reader, may develop an approach in which soft areas merge with soft areas and there is an absence of the need to control the structure in this way. Out of

106 *Opposite:* Tapestry: 'Nomads' village',
167 cm × 120 cm (5 ft 6 in × 4 ft)

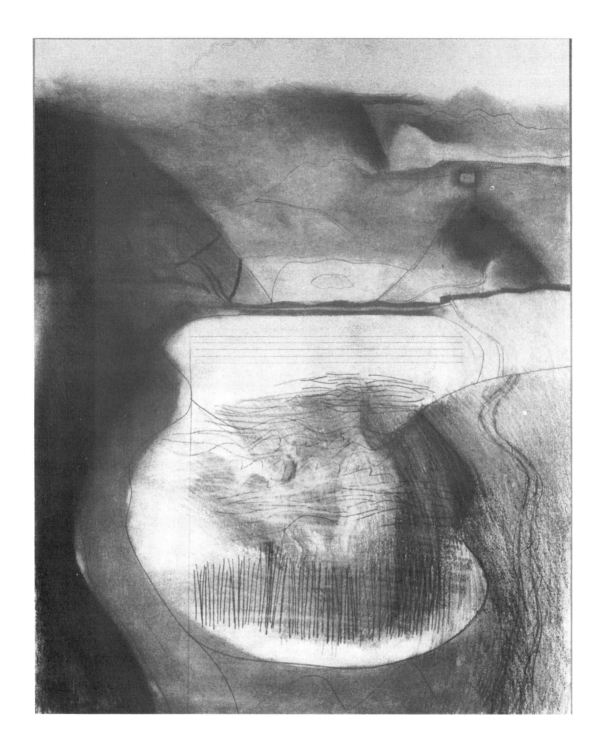

107 Drawing: 'Tarn on a hill'

108 *Opposite*: Tapestry: 'Black fells', 152 cm × 120 cm (5 ft × 4 ft)

109 *Opposite*: Tapestry:
'Sea and islands',
180 cm × 120 cm
(6 ft × 4 ft)

110 Detail of 'Sea and islands'

105

these differences individual styles grow. While this book urges you to think and design in clear shapes and to avoid a sloppy use of texture, it is recognised that a reasonable reaction to this advice from someone who is temperamentally different from the writer would be to attach less importance to clear structure and to build up the work in a more nebulous manner.

Figure 111. 'Variations on a tarn'

Figure 112. 'Genesis 1:2'
These two tapestries use the saucer-like shapes seen in previous examples above, but they are used in different ways. Figure 112 was planned carefully, as it had to be a special size for a wall in a chapel. The dark, heavily-textured void of the lower section is echoed in a still, striped saucer section and re-echoed in an undulating saucer shape, which meets on the surface of the waters the definite downward thrust of the colourful and more agitated area. The white V-shape at the top emphasises the downward direction, but is related to a calm hilltop, which is a religious mountain image.

Figure 111 was spontaneously woven. It combines aggressive, jagged shapes with softer undulations and has five variations on a tarn theme. The colour is dominatingly red. Texture in both pieces is, as usual, limited. In the middle variation of figure 111 there are small areas of fine horizontals. The colours of two adjacent areas cross into each other's territory. (That is, one pick across returns to make two picks. The opposite colour is built up and then performs the same move across.) The resulting striped shape can be drawn out on the warp as the weaving proceeds. Figure 29 illustrates this technique. It was used in several other small areas but, as the tones are very close, it is difficult to pick them out in a black and white photograph.

Figure 113. 'Wood in Cumbria 2'
A later version of figure 82, the basic layout was drawn on the warp and reference was made to a photograph of figure 82 (as the original tapestry had been sold some time previously). The photo-graph was then put away and the weaving developed within the framework, but with a different emphasis in almost every part. So although a number of tapestries may look superficially alike, in fact each is an original piece.

Figure 114. Drawing
This small sketch was a starting point for the tapestry, 'Village in hills'. In the event, an additional line of hills was included, among other changes, and the tapestry was considerably smaller than the one envisaged. It is a good idea to keep small sketches and jottings. This particular one is still in reserve, after several years, because the theme and the layout are of continuing interest and might form the stimulus for a big tapestry at some future date.

Finishing and hanging

Before cutting off the loom check that there are no alterations to be made. Cutting out to make corrections has already been referred to. Because of the restrictions in opening the sheds, any corrections have to be filled in with needle weaving. A tapestry needle, bent at the end, is threaded carefully through the warp ends. The number of picks must be matched exactly and care must be taken to count the steps. If this is done without haste the corrected piece will be indistinguishable from the rest of the weaving.

When the top hem has been woven (if so required), slacken the warp and, with sharp shears or scissors, cut the tapestry off the loom. Leave from 15 cm to 30 cm (6 in to 1 ft) of warp projecting at each end of the work. If the work is to be hemmed it should first be knotted against the weft. Take the warp ends in pairs and knot them so that the knot can be pushed evenly against the weft all along the edge (see figure 115). Then turn the hem and stitch along, being careful not to go right through the thickness of the tapestry or to pull the stitching thread so tight that the hem becomes uneven and tight. The warp ends should be trimmed, but not too near the knots in case some retying is necessary at a later date (see figure 116).

111 Tapestry: 'Variations on a tarn', 180 cm × 153 cm
(6 ft × 5 ft)

112 Tapestry: 'Genesis 1:2', 148 cm × 126 cm (4 ft 10 in × 4 ft 2 in)

113 *Opposite*: Tapestry: 'Wood in Cumbria 2', 165 cm × 120 cm (5 ft 5 in × 4 ft)

114 Small drawing for a tapestry

115 Overhand knotting for a fringe

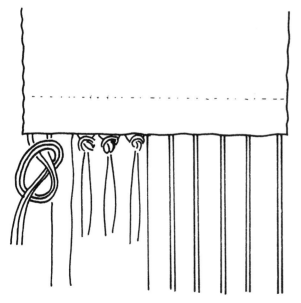

116 Hemming

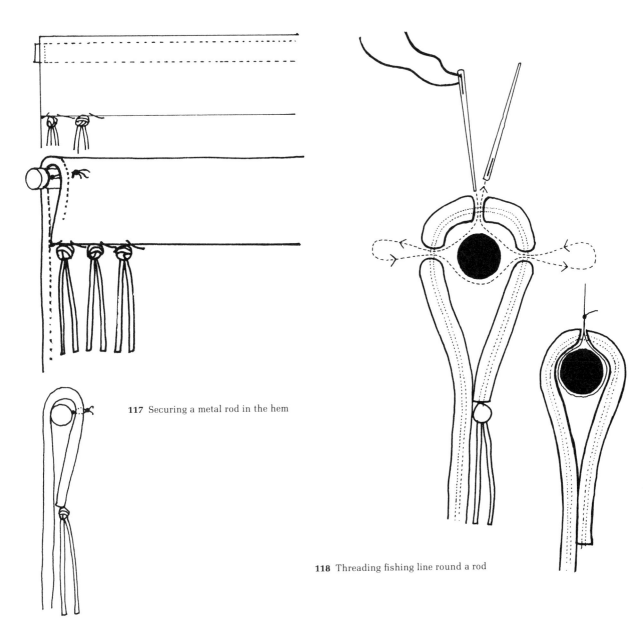

117 Securing a metal rod in the hem

118 Threading fishing line round a rod

The bottom edge can be left knotted as a fringe, without a hem, but only if this is really in sympathy with the work. It is best to keep the finishing as simple as possible.

The width of the hem will have been calculated to take a steel or wooden rod or an aluminium strip. If the tapestry is to be handled often in transit or at exhibitions, and there is a danger of the rod falling out, file a groove at each end of the rod near to the end and tie a strong thin thread round the groove. Stitch it to the adjacent warp towards the top back of the hem (figure 117). Use transparent fishing line filament to attach strings to the rod (at three points for a 120 cm (4 ft) width). The filament should go round the rod and out at the top of the hem. Use a blunt needle, entering and leaving at the same points, until the filament can be pulled freely round the rod (figure 118). In doing this operation be careful not to entangle the weft

111

fibres in the filament. It is very easy after a few attempts. Knot at a point near the top of the tapestry, tie a loop at the end of the filament and when all are completed hang from fine wall nails (figure 119). A variation, which conceals the hanging points, consists of fixing three stainless steel nails into the wall. The heads of the nails are nipped off either before or after fixing, so that the tapestry can be pressed against the nails and the rod will rest comfortably on the nails. It helps if the nails slope slightly upwards as in figure 120.

In the case of an aluminium strip drill two or three holes near the top edge. (Two holes should be equidistant in a short length of aluminium;

119 Hanging a tapestry with fishing line

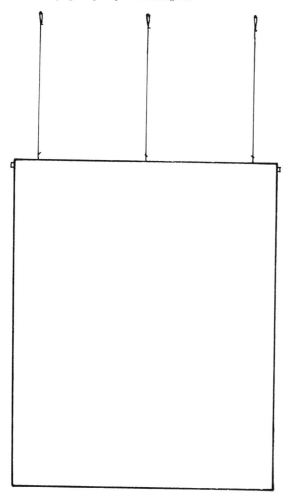

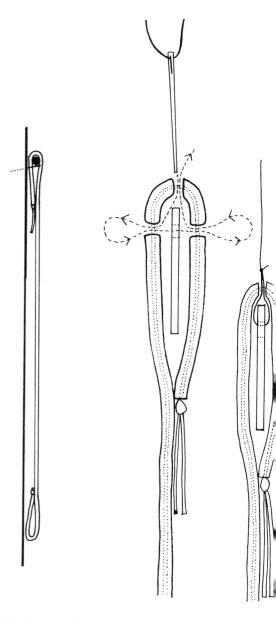

120 *Left*: Concealed hanging on stainless steel nails

121 *Right*: Threading fishing line through aluminium strip

three holes should have one in the middle of the length and the other two equidistant 5 cm to 10 cm (2 in to 4 in) from the ends.)

As the position of the holes can be measured accurately on the tapestry when the aluminium strip is inside the hem, it is easy to thread a filament through (see figure 121) in such a way that it is fixed round inside the hole and emerges at the top of the hem, as in the case of the rod. To make a concealed hanging, stainless steel nails should be fixed in the wall to coincide with holes. The tapestry can then be pressed onto the nails as in figure 122.

If the work is being sent to an exhibition the fishing line method of hanging is preferable to the concealed method. The filament line should be long enough to reach the top of the gallery wall, so that those who are responsible for hanging can make adjustments without the need to rethread. If it is not clear to a third party that a tapestry should hang in a particular way, some galleries improvise destructive methods of suspending the work. This is not always their fault.

When the bottom edge has been knotted and hemmed and the warp ends trimmed, they sometimes hang below the bottom of the tapestry. Gather them in groups and sew along the line of the hem (figure 123). If there are no hems the tapestry can be finished in the following ways.

When using single warp ends, turn each end down into the space between the next warp end along and the weft. Use a needle, and thread the warp down for about 5 cm (2 in) before bringing it out at the back. Trim the end, leaving about 2 cm ($\frac{3}{4}$ in) showing, as in figure 124. This makes a very neat finish. There is, however, one disadvantage: the thickening of the edge, as the ends are threaded down, tends to pull the weft and to make the tapestry narrower.

In the case of double warp ends, take alternate single ends (that is, one from each double end) and thread them down the next warp end along, in turn. Then fold back the remaining single ends and stitch them down. Although this looks very neat and regular it also has the disadvantage of tightening the weft (see figure 125). If the weft is woven slightly slacker for the last 8 cm (3 in) or so, to compensate for this tightening effect, a perfect result is possible.

In order to hang a tapestry which has been finished in this way, sew a length of Velcro (touch-and-close fastener) 4 cm or 5 cm ($1\frac{1}{2}$ in or 2 in) in width along the edge of the work. Stick the corresponding length of Velcro (with the

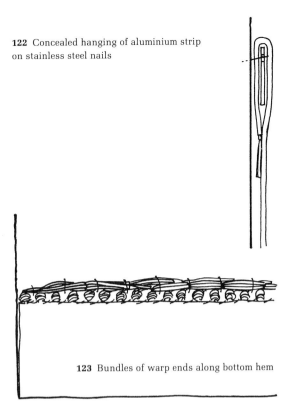

122 Concealed hanging of aluminium strip on stainless steel nails

123 Bundles of warp ends along bottom hem

124 Single warp ends threaded down adjacent warp ends

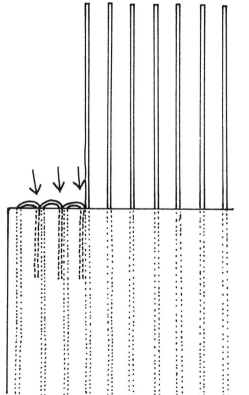

113

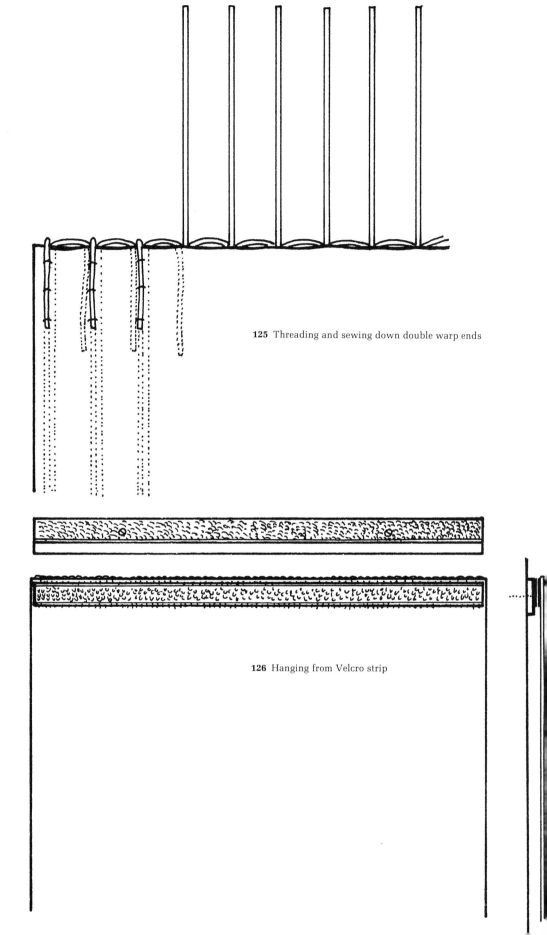

125 Threading and sewing down double warp ends

126 Hanging from Velcro strip

127 Back view of tapestry showing webbing in position,
with section showing position of wooden laths inside
webbing sleeve

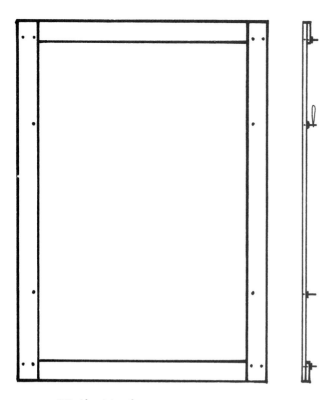

128 Aluminium frame

hooked finish) to a piece of wood, well seasoned, $5\,cm \times 1\,cm$ or $0.5\,cm$ $(2\,in \times \frac{1}{2}\,in$ or $\frac{1}{4}\,in) \times$ the width of the tapestry. Hang this on the wall, before fixing the tapestry to it, by pressing the lengths of Velcro to each other (see figure 126). It is advisable to strengthen the back edges of the sides of tapestries by sewing lengths of webbing down each edge at the back of the work. If the webbing is $5\,cm$ $(2\,in)$ wide, stitch it closely along the edge of the tapestry and then sew the other edge of the webbing less closely. Turn the ends of the webbing in, stitch the bottom end, but leave the top end open. In some positions, where the tapestry might be handled and pulled out of shape, it is an advantage to have a sleeve of webbing into which a wooden lath can slide (figure 127). With or without the lath, the webbing is essential, unless the tapestry is to remain in one place on a wall where no one will be tempted to turn it over and pull it out of shape in an effort to see just how it is made.

116

Sometimes it is advisable to stretch the tapestry, or rather to fix it so that all the edges are controlled and stuck to a support. Make a frame the same size as the tapestry, from $5\,cm \times \frac{1}{2}\,cm$ $(2\,in \times \frac{1}{4}\,in)$ aluminium strips (figure 128). The corners are best screwed together with small nuts and bolts. The bolts are countersunk. Additional bolts are fitted at intervals along the uprights to hold the frame $1\,cm$ $(\frac{1}{2}\,in)$ away from the wall. Attach a wire loop to the back of the bolts marked A, shown in figure 129. These loops fit easily over picture hooks. Glue lengths of Velcro (hooked surface) along the front edges of the uprights and the back edges of the cross pieces, using an impact adhesive on a clean and slightly roughened surface. Scratch the metal surface to give the adhesive some tooth to hold on to. Figure 129 shows the Velcro in position on the front of the uprights, with an accompanying side elevation showing it in position on the back edge of the cross pieces.

The tapestry must have a $5\,cm$ $(2\,in)$ hem, top and bottom, for this method to be effective. Stitch Velcro (looped surface) on all the back edges of the work. It is easy to attach the tapestry to the frame, starting with the top, folding it over and pressing the Velcro lengths together and then easing it down the sides and round the bottom edge. As the Velcro comes away with gentle pulling, adjustments are made smoothly until the tapestry hangs quite naturally on the frame. Avoid too much pulling and stretching. The finished work, in place, should look very much like the tapestry before it was cut off the loom.

Variations on this method are sometimes desirable. For example, with a large hanging it is sometimes best to fix lengths of wood on the wall to coincide with the size of the tapestry. The sides and the bottom are fronted with Velcro. The tapestry is hemmed and the top hem has within it an aluminium strip, with a series of holes in measured positions. Before the tapestry is adjusted along the edges it is screwed to the top length of wood through the holes in the aluminium. The screws should be stainless steel or brass. The heads of the screws

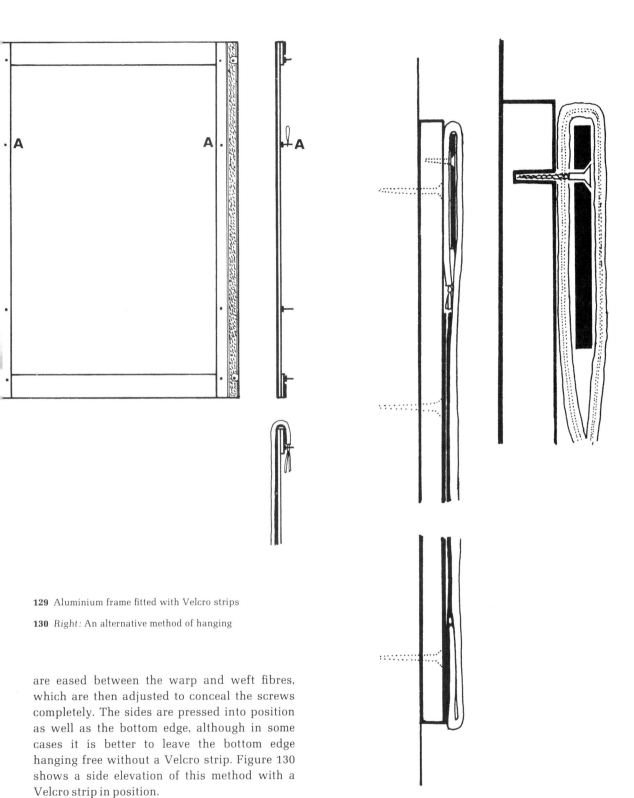

129 Aluminium frame fitted with Velcro strips

130 *Right:* An alternative method of hanging

are eased between the warp and weft fibres, which are then adjusted to conceal the screws completely. The sides are pressed into position as well as the bottom edge, although in some cases it is better to leave the bottom edge hanging free without a Velcro strip. Figure 130 shows a side elevation of this method with a Velcro strip in position.

4 TAPESTRIES 'IN SITU'

Mural paintings, mosaics, ceramic murals, wooden reliefs, sculpted reliefs, textile constructions and tapestries can, singly or in combination, fundamentally change the architectural space in a building. Like framed paintings, they can be self-contained, but not entirely so, because the nature of the materials in use and the deliberately planned areas which they occupy make them an essential part of an overall setting. A tapestry, while being flat and pictorial, has much in common with carpets, curtains and other furnishing materials. If it is not chosen carefully for the setting, or specially designed for it, it can look more disastrously wrong than any framed picture of a similar size in the same position.

The three tapestries which are illustrated in the section which follows were all commissioned for a particular space. Some of the problems are described.

Figure 131. 'Midlands landscape'
The building was not finished when the commission was given, but the relevant wall was standing and it was possible to visualise the position of the large reception desk. Colour samples of furnishing fabrics and floor finishes were provided by the architect. After seeing the building there was a period of a month or so in which three sets of drawings and colour diagrams were prepared on the theme of Midlands landscapes. The motivating factor

was a wish, on the part of the clients, that the tapestry should not be abstract, but should have some relationship to the landscape elements which would be familiar to those using the building. The size was to be 180 cm × 360 cm (6 ft × 12 ft). After discussion, however, it was agreed that an extra 30 cm (1 ft) on the height would be useful, so that the tapestry could be hung so that the bottom edge was below the top of the reception desk. Because of the size of the loom in use it was agreed that there should be a 240 cm (8 ft) wide middle panel, and two 75 cm (2 ft 6 in) side panels, stitched on the vertical join. The side panels were designed to range from white, through greys, to blacks, from top to bottom in one case and bottom to top in the other. Browns, reds, pinks and golds were to dominate the middle panel, to form a strong focus complementing the red of the furniture in the centre of the reception area. When finished, the top edge was hemmed, fitted with an aluminium strip and screwed to a length of wood which was already screwed to the wall. Lengths of wood faced with Velcro were screwed to the wall to coincide with the sides of the tapestry, which also had Velcro sewn on. The edges were carefully aligned. The bottom hem was left hanging freely.

Figure 132. Two tapestries at the Guildhall School of Music and Drama, London

118

The building was standing but not finished. The solid monolithic concrete demanded colour. The basic idea came from sventeenth-century engravings of the City of London and the river. The tapestries were commissioned by the School, with the help of the Radcliffe Trust and the Worshipful Company of Dyers. There was early agreement that the interpretation of the architectural features in the engravings could be freely interpreted and developed. It was decided to make the colour rich and the effect decorative and strongly patterned, running through white, grey, reds, pinks and browns in that sort of order from top to bottom in one tapestry, and in the same sort of order from bottom to top in the other. There were problems about the size and about the exact height for hanging. The spherical lights about 240 cm (8 ft) from the floor were fixtures, so it was decided finally to hang with the bottom edge of the

131 Tapestry: 'Midlands landscape', in reception hall, IBM Midlands Centre, Warwick. 210 cm × 360 cm (7 ft × 12 ft)

tapestries at the same height as the lights. This would also have the effect of putting the tapestries just beyond the reach of most hands. Because there was no chance, in normal circumstances, of the tapestries being handled, they were both hung from three wire loops, fitted to aluminium strips. There was no webbing on the back edges, but aluminium strips were thought to be necessary in the bottom hems. They hang in a busy foyer much used by students. The concrete walls give off a certain amount of dust and it is, therefore, necessary to vacuum the surfaces carefully from time to time, in order to retain the freshness of the colour and to preserve the wool. There is little daylight, so spots are in use most of the time.

*Figure 133. Tapestry at Equitable Life
Assurance Society, London*

The building had been standing for some time,
but the reception area was being redesigned. A
terrazzo mosaic surfaced wall faced the lifts,
and the problem was to relieve the surface in
some way. A tapestry would need to suggest
space, depth and light. It was decided to use a
northern moorland theme, with a deep red
central area and an emphasis on sky and
distant hills at the top. Because of its position,
it was supported using the method outlined
under figure 131.

132 *Opposite*: Tapestries in foyer, Guildhall School of
Music and Drama, Barbican, London. Each 330 cm × 240 cm
(11 ft × 8 ft)

The time-table, for all three groups of tapestries
described above, was similar:

1 Initial viewing of building. Discussion with
architect, or architect and client.

2 Period to prepare two or three drawings and
colour samples. This can vary, depending on the
urgency of the commission, from a week to
several weeks.

3 Meeting to explain drawings and colour
schemes to architect or client, or to both. This
can be done by post in the case of an individual
patron. In the above examples there were
meetings and discussions.

After the designs were accepted the work was
commissioned at an agreed price, for delivery at

121

an agreed date. The date depends on two factors:

1 The date when the building will be ready for the tapestry.

2 The speed of weaving, calculated on about one to two weeks for setting up the loom, dyeing, or buying special colours, plus 900 square cm (1 square ft) per working day, allowing for five working days per seven day week, or under pressure, for a seven day working week, plus up to two weeks for cutting off and finishing.

Whether the tapestry is being designed for a public building, or for a friend's house, certain points should be considered:

1 What is the ideal size of tapestry for the space?

2 What colours dominate the space, or the room, already?

3 Does the architect, client, or friend have ideas on themes? How far do you take these into consideration in preparing drawings? This is most important. It depends on how much you like to interact with someone else's ideas.

4 As a designer/weaver, your method of working might need explaining. For example, a client may ask for a painting which will show exactly what the tapestry will look like. Do you agree to this? Or do you explain that drawing gives the layout, that a colour diagram and/or

122

wool samples suggest the basic colours, but that it is only possible to see what the work looks like when it has been woven, because the originality of the work lies in the development of the weaving. It is usually reassuring to a client if the designer can produce an agreed basic layout in pencil and stick to it. But it should be borne in mind that for many people the idea of using skilled weaving techniques to copy or even interpret a painting is quite acceptable. The extent to which an individual designer-weaver may deviate from this needs very patient explanation, and an understanding of the client's role.

134 & 135 Tapestries in an exhibition in Schloss Rheydt Museum, Germany

Lighting

Tapestries should never hang in direct sunlight or in strong daylight. Flood or spot lights are ideally placed well out in front, and above, so as not to over emphasise the texture of the weave, unless this is the intention. Good indirect daylight should be supplemented where possible with occasional artificial lighting, which can bring out the richness of colours. It is not necessary to light the whole tapestry evenly, unless there is a wish to do so, in which case it is possible to have light which lights only the surface and nothing of the surrounding areas.

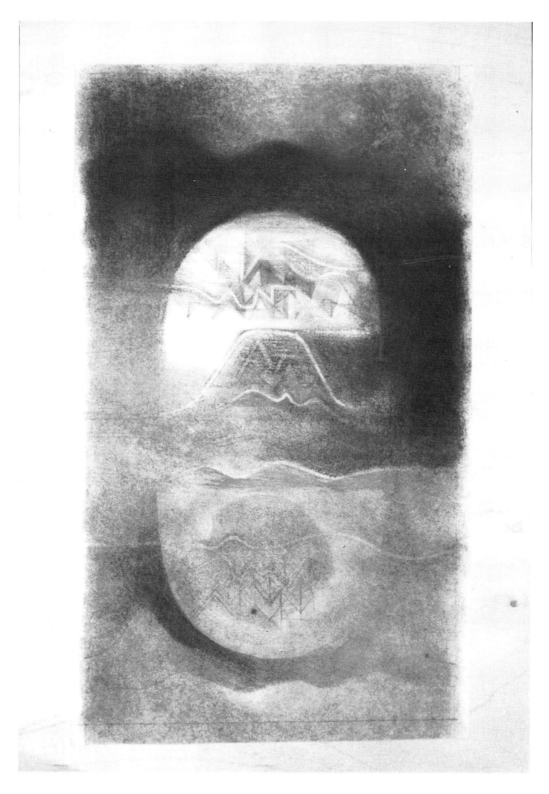

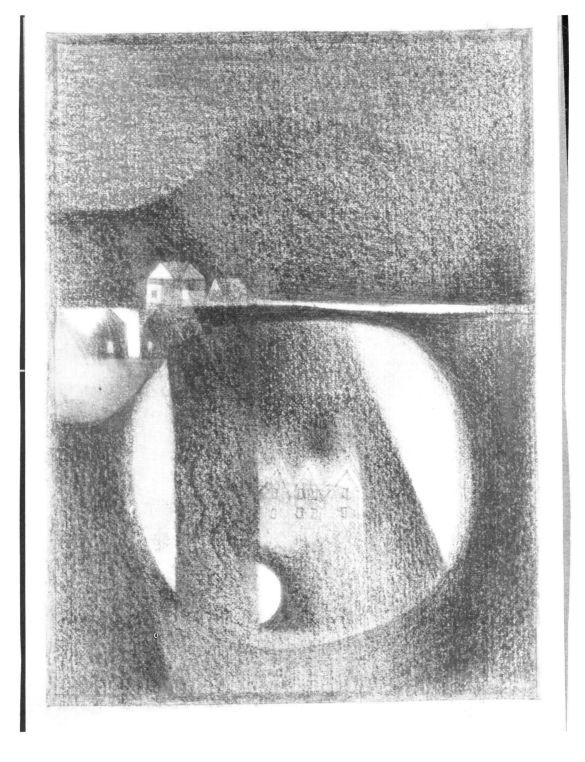

136 *Opposite*: Drawing: 'Small island'   137 Drawing: 'Houses by a tarn'

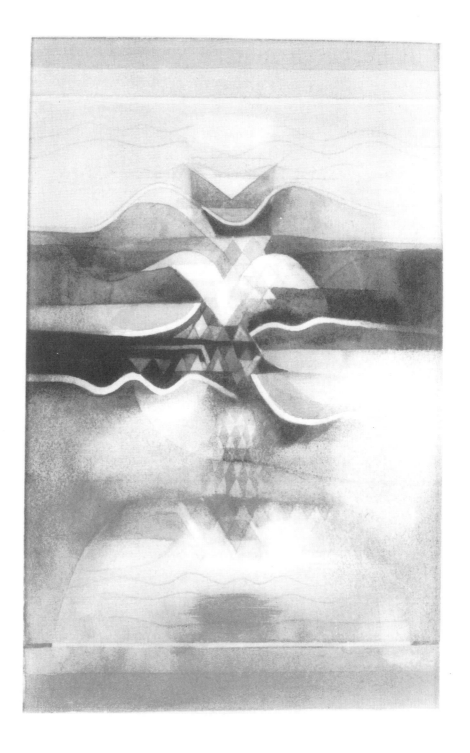

138 *Opposite*: Watercolour study for tapestry, 'Roads into a village' (see figure 70)

139 Tapestry: 'Path in the sky over Cumbria', 150 cm × 120 cm (4 ft 11 in × 4 ft)

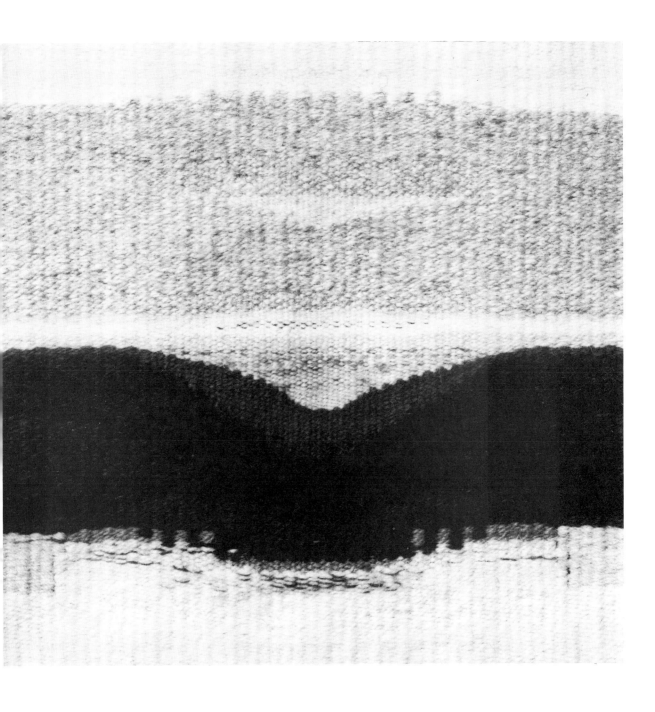

140 *Opposite*: Tapestry: 'Lake, rising above the trees (an 'I Ching' theme), 150 cm × 120 cm (4 ft 11 in × 4 ft)

141 Small tapestry in which middle areas are set at eight warp ends per 2.5 cm (1 in) and the rest at four double ends per 2.5 cm (1 in)

GLOSSARY

Beater Wooden or metal tool, made on the principle of the comb, for pressing down the weft. It is best to use fingers, or a bobbin point, at first and to do without a beater, unless it really appears to be necessary to beat the weft down very hard.

Bobbin Wooden spool for holding weft yarn. The point is also useful for pressing down the weft.

Cartoon A design drawn to scale, for a tapestry, mural painting, mosaic or other work of art.

End A single warp thread.

Finger-shedding A way of making the shed with the fingers, which raise alternating ends to facilitate the passage of the weft.

G-clamp G-shaped metal clamp.

Hank Circular loop or coil (of woollen yarn).

Haute lisse A tapestry woven on a vertical or high warp loom.

Leash A single loop of string or cord which passes round an end and a leash bar and which is pulled by the weaver to make the shed.

Pass A tapestry-weaving term for two picks.

Pick A single weft thread. In tapestry-weaving terms this is a half pass.

Return A personal way of describing two picks or a pass. Two picks or a pass build up the steps in weaving a shape. As the step is made of a pick which returns around a warp end, it has become a habit in my studio to describe a step as being made of three, four returns, and so on.

Selvedge The side edge of the tapestry, formed by the first and last warp ends. Some weavers recommend that these ends should be thicker than the rest of the warp. This is acceptable if a slightly thicker edge is required. Any additional thickness in an end shows in the weaving of the weft. The selvedge can also be made firmer if the weft is, from time to time, given an extra turn around the selvedge warp ends.

Shed The opening of the warp, through which the weft passes. In tapestry weaving there are only two sheds.

Skein A bundle of yarn made by coiling. A handskein or finger skein is made by coiling the yarn round the finger and thumb in such a way that the yarn can be drawn out without tangling the skein.

Step A literal step by which the weft is built up from warp end to warp end to form a shape in the tapestry.

Warp Threads running lengthways on the loom, which are completely covered by the weft in traditional tapestry weaving.

Weft Threads woven across the loom and the warp.

Weft-faced A fabric, like tapestry, in which the warp is entirely covered by the weft.

BIBLIOGRAPHY

BEUTLICH, Tadek, *The technique of Woven Tapestry*, Batsford, 1967.

CONSTANTINE, Mildred and LARSON, Jack Lenor, *The Art Fabric: Mainstream*, Van Nostrand Reinhold, 1973.

GEIJER, Agnes, *A History of Textile Art*, Sotheby Parke Bernet, 1979.

GILBY, Myriam, *Free Weaving*, Pitman, 1976.

GOODWIN, Jill, *A Dyer's Manual*, Pelham Books, 1982.

d'HARCOURT, Raoul, *Textiles of Ancient Peru and their Techniques*, University of Washington Press, 1966.

HORSFALL, R. S. and LAWRIE, L. G. *The Dyeing of Textile Fibres*, Chapman and Hall, 1946.

KAUFMANN, Ruth, *The New American Tapestry*, Reinhold Book Corporation, New York, 1968.

LARSON, Jack Lenor, *The Dyer's Art: Ikat, Batik and Plangi*, Van Nostrand Reinhold, 1977.

LURÇAT, Jean, *Designing Tapestry*, Rockliff, 1950.

MOORMAN, Theo, *Weaving as an Art Form*, Van Nostrand Reinhold, 1975.

PICTON, John and MACK, John, *African Textiles*, British Museum Publications, 1979.

REDMAN, Jane, *Frame-loom Weaving*, Van Nostrand Reinhold, 1976.

SUTTON, Ann, COLLINGWOOD, Peter, St AUBYN HUBBARD, Geraldine, *The Craft of the Weaver*, British Broadcasting Corporation, 1982.

THOMSON, F. P. *Tapestry—Mirror of History*, David and Charles, 1980.

TIDBALL, Harriet, *Contemporary Tapestry*, Shuttle Craft Monograph Twelve, 1964. Distributed by Craft and Hobby Service, Big Sur, California.

VERLET, Pierre, FLORISOONE, Michel, HOFFMEISTER, Adolf, *The Book of Tapestry*, Octupus Books, 1978.

WALLER, Irene, *Fine Art Weaving*, Batsford, 1979.

WALLER, Irene, *Textile Sculptures*, Studio Vista, 1977.

WASSEF, R. W. and FORMAN, W., *Tapestries from Egypt*, Hamlyn, 1968.

WASSEF, R. W. and FORMAN, W., *Woven by Hand*, Hamlyn, 1973.

SUPPLIERS

UK

Looms, frames

The Edinburgh Tapestry Co.
Dovecot Studios, Dovecot Rd
Edinburgh, EH12 7LE

Harris Looms
Northgrove Road, Hawkhurst
Kent, TN18 4AP

Dryad
Northgates
Leicester

Warp and weft materials

Craftsman's Mark Ltd
Tone Dale Mill
Wellington
Somerset, TA21 0AW (linen warp, 2/5s rug yarn)

'Yarns'
21 Portland St
Taunton
Somerset

A. K. Graupner
Corner House
Valley Rd
Bradford, BD1 4AA

Weavers' Shop
Royal Wilton Carpet Factory
Wilton
Wilts.

Handweavers Studio and Gallery Ltd
29 Haroldstone Road
London W17 7AN

The Yarn Store
89A Grosvenor Avenue,
Highbury
London N5 2NL

Susan Foster
9 Windermere Road
Kendal
Cumbria

Dyes

Boots Chemists

Chemists and hardware stores

Also for a controlled chemical dyeing process:

The Russell Dye System
Muswell Hill Weavers
65 Roseberry Road
London N10 2LE

Artists' materials

Reeves & Sons Ltd
Lincoln Rd
Enfield
Middlesex

George Rowney & Co Ltd
10 Percy St
London W1

Winsor & Newton Ltd
51 Rathbone Place
London W1

USA

Looms, frames

Edward Bosworth
132 Indian Creek Rd
Ithaca
New York, 14850

Bexel Handlooms
2470 Dixie Highway
Pontiac
Michigan, 48055

Gilmore Looms
1032 North Broadway Avenue
Stockton
California 95205

Yarns and dyes

Countryside Handweavers
Box 1225
Mission
Kansas 66222

Yarns

Shuttlecraft
PO Box 6041
Providence
Rhode Island, 02940

Old Mill Yarn
PO Box 115, Eaton Rapids
Michigan 48827

Contessa Yarns
PO Box 37
Lebanon
Connecticut 06249

American Thread Corporation
90 Park Avenue
New York, 10016

Mail Order

American Handicraft Co.
20 West 14th St
New York, 10011

The Thread Shed
307 Freeport Rd
Pittsburgh
Pennsylvania 15215

Australia

Spinning and weaving suppliers who accept mail orders:

Several Arts
63 Jersey Rd
Woolahra
New South Wales 2025

Spin and Weave
Room 16, First Floor
Centreway Arcade
Launceston
Tasmania 7250

Arty and Crafty
484 Goodwood Rd
Cumberland Park
South Australia 5041

Village Weaver
29 Stirling Highway
Nedlands
Western Australia 6009

Wondoflex Yarn Crafts Pty Ltd
1353 Malvern Rd
Malvern
Victoria 3144

USEFUL ADDRESSES

UK

Association of Guilds of Weavers, Spinners and Dyers, BCM 963, London WC1N 3XX. Publication: *Weavers Journal*, four issues for Annual Subscription, from The Secretary, The Weavers Journal, address as above. From this address a list of local Guild secretaries can be obtained, and a booklet which gives a useful list of suppliers of materials.

Crafts Council, 12 Waterloo Place, London SW1Y 4AU. Telephone: 01-930 4811. Publishes *Crafts* magazine, bi-monthly. Has exhibition gallery, slide collection, information and publications.

USA

The American Crafts Council, 29 West 53rd Street, New York 10019. Has information on craft organisations and courses. Publication: *Craft Horizon*, bi-monthly.

Australia

Crafts Council of Australia, 27 King Street, Sidney 2000. There is an Exhibition office, Publications office and Resource Centre. Publication: *Craft Australia*.

Craft Associations in each State and Territory have special groups in many cities and country towns. Useful addresses for weavers are:

Canberra Spinners and Weavers, PO Box 1452, Canberra City 2601.

The Handweavers' and Spinners' Guild of Australia, GPO Box 67, Sydney 2001.

Queensland Spinners, Weavers and Dyers Group, c/o J. Grant-Taylor, 550 Lutwych Road, Lutwych 4030.

Handspinners and Weavers Guild, c/o 6 Alma Street, Panorama 5041.

Handweavers, Spinners and Dyers Guild of Burnie, c/o PO Box 194, Somerset 7322.

Handweavers, Spinners and Dyers Guild of Launceston, c/o J. McLaughlan, 'Tam-o-Shanter', Weymouth 7252.

Handweavers, Spinners and Dyers Guild of Tasmania, PO Box 115, North Hobart 7002.

Handweavers and Spinners Guild of Victoria, 31 Victoria Street, Melbourne 3000.

Handweavers and Spinners Guild of W.A., PO Box 171, Claremont 6010.

INDEX